THE HOTTEST SUMMER EVER

ELIJAH R. FREEMAN

URBAN AINT DEAD PRESENTS

CONTENTS

URBAN AINT DEAD

P.O Box 960780

Riverdale GA., 30296

Copyright © 2021 By Elijah R. Freeman

All rights reserved. Published by URBAN AINT DEAD Publications.

Cover Design: Nicole Watts / **Kreations K** www.kreationsk.com

Edited & Interior Design: Bianca Shakur / **B. Edits** www.editwithb.com

URBAN AINT DEAD and coinciding logo(s) are registered properties.

Contact the Author at www.freemanreads.com.

Contact Publisher at www.urbanaintdead.com

Email: urbanaintdead@gmail.com

Print ISBN: 978-1-7355238-2-8

Ebook ISBN: 978-1-7355238-3-5

Urban Aint Dead: Like our page on Facebook:
www.facebook.com/urbanaintdead
&
Follow us on Instagram:
@urbanaintdead

SUBMISSION GUIDELINES

Submit the first three chapters of your completed manuscript to urbanaintdead@gmail.com, subject line: Your book's title. The manuscript must be in a .doc file and sent as an attachment. The document should be in Times New Roman, double-spaced and in size 12 font. Also, provide your synopsis and full contact information. If sending multiple submissions, they must each be in a separate email.

Have a story but no way to submit it electronically? You can still submit to **URBAN AINT DEAD.** Send in the first three chapters, written or typed, of your completed manuscript to:

URBAN AINT DEAD
P.O Box 960780
Riverdale GA., 30296
DO NOT send original manuscript. Must be a duplicate.

Provide your synopsis and a cover letter containing your full
contact information
Thanks for considering **URBAN AINT DEAD**

ACKNOWLEDGMENTS

Yooo, waddup, world!? Off top, I gotta give thanks to Allah, whom without, none of this is possible. So all praise to him. This has been one heck of a journey, but he has brought me far and has blessed me with numerous followers in the process. To everyone who is reading this, whether you've followed my work from the beginning or this is the first book you've read by me...thank you.

I wanna say thanks to my mama and fiancé for being my biggest supporters. Y'all are my real Days Ones. I Love y'all with everything in me. In some way or another y'all have played a huge part in my success. Thanks for seeing the Greatness in me even when it got hard to see it for myself. On those dark nights when I wanted to give up, I couldn't see myself letting y'all down. I fought through it. Now, here we are: Book five and URBAN AINT DEAD.

Much Love to everyone who helped me piece this project together: Bianca Shakur at B. Edits for the A-1 editing, Nicole

Watts at Kreations K for the dope book cover, and my longtime writing mentor, Thomas Habersham, for giving me a better understanding of The Elements of Fiction.

Shout-out to T-Bo DaVip and Reemarkable for the phenomenal single we put together for this novel. To everyone who supports me, go to your choice streaming service and run them streams through the roof!!! The single is titled "The Hottest Summer Ever" by T-Bo DaVip featuring Reemarkable and its out now on all platforms so y'all be sure to check that out, and while you're at it be sure to check out other novel soundtracks and singles released by URBAN AINT DEAD.

Big ups to Lockdown Publication C.E.O CA$H for inspiring me to write as a juvenile and for being a beacon of hope to incarcerated authors everywhere. You give so much to Urban Fiction, and through it all you remain humble. Salute!

Special thanks to Kendra Black, the dopest Virtual Assistant in the game. With each task you make me think in new directions, and make what I do so much easier. You're very much appreciated.

And finally, I wanna give a BIG thank you to Sister Souljah for penning my all-time favorite Urban Fiction novel, "The Coldest Winter Ever." I hope you don't take this the wrong way, but the story is so inspiring. Till this day, I can read it over and over and it never gets old. Your pen game is legendary. It takes real craft to connect readers to characters the way we feel about Winter and her co-stars. And now, being an author myself, I have an even greater respect for what you did with those characters. Writing isn't as easy as most people believe, but we Love what we do.

The original name of this book was *All Work, No Play*. At the time, I was eighteen and in the hole at Eastman YDC, and the story wasn't what it is now. I changed the title to *Platinum Kush* when I was twenty, and again to *To Live With No One To Love* when I was twenty-two. The title it bears now came to me when I decided to put it out under my own company, URBAN AINT DEAD.

While in the process of writing the final version, I altered the plot. In the end, I found that the protagonist's pain mirrored my own. This is a story of betrayal. It was written at a period of my life when I was at my lowest, and despite the handful of people I had in my corner, I felt alone.

If you don't take anything from this story, remember this: if your real enemies don't get you, your fake friends will.

Anyone can stand by someone when they're up, but it takes a special person to be there when you're down. Who would've thought your love and support would turn out to be the motivational force behind my success. Thanks for always having my back.
I Love you, Monesa.

PROLOGUE

Reluctant

Lighting flashed, thunder boomed and heavy rain pelted the top of the stolen Toyota Corolla as I made my way home. Feeling like time was working against me, I pushed the car past the speed limit, throwing caution to the wind. I was in a lot of pain. The adrenaline rush from my mission had subsided and the wear and tear on my shoulder was catching up to me. There was no time to acknowledge pain though. More imperative issues were on my mind. Like why Keisha hadn't told us about the unexpected visit that caused her not to eradicate all traces left by the crew. We could have done damage control before things had gotten this far.

Everyone was dead now. No wonder Keisha had backed out of the streets to go legit. She was running from her past. Her karma. Yet it found her. Her, Redd and Polo; and there was still a loose end unattended. A loose end with all the answers to my remaining questions but would create new problems. Seeing who I'd just seen moments ago reminded me just how small the world really was. It also reiterated the fact that anything was possible and to always expect the unexpected. That along with my knowledge of Zoepound and the little I remember of what Keisha disclosed about them confirmed my suspicions and broke my heart at the same time. Redd was right.

I pulled into the driveway and sat there, trying to fix myself up in an attempt to stop the pain, physical and emotional. It was 4 am. I didn't want to do it but I grabbed my strap. My life was damaged beyond repair. Chelsea was the single thread that held it together. Without her, my whole world would fall apart. What was the point in having money if there was no one to share it with? No one from the bottom to look back with from the top. I'd spend the rest of my life in question. Wondering if the people around me loved me for me, or simply for what I could do for them. That's no way for a woman to live. A lot could've been different, and staring at the gun in my hands, all the mistakes I made throughout life came rushing back...

CHAPTER ONE

CRUSHED DREAMS

B orn and raised in College Park, it's no surprise that I turned out to be a product of my environment. I was born to Richard and Nicole Love on March 28th, 1990 at Grady Memorial, one of Georgia's prominent hospitals. At the last minute before signing my birth certificate they decided on a name, Richelle Kemoni Love. Then a few days after I was pronounced healthy, my mother was discharged and they were finally able to take me home to our small apartment on Godby Road.

I was daddy's little girl. Whatever I wanted, I got. I loved my mama, but me and daddy just always had a deeper relationship. Daddy felt children were smarter than what a lot of people gave them credit for. As a result, he spoke to me as if I was a lot older than I actually was. I was always with him, even when he would stop by some of his stash houses. He never sheltered me from what was going on, and because of this, I grew up more advanced than most kids in my neighborhood. For me, there was no Santa Clause, Easter bunny or Prince Charming. It was just daddy, my knight in shining armor. He was my everything. His every movement was geared towards providing for me and mama, and to give me the life he never had. For a while he did. My daddy, my uncle Ron, and their childhood friend, Big Rod had found a plug and was on the come up. Then one night everything changed.

I was nine when my daddy was killed. He was just starting to make a name for himself in the dope trade. The competition felt the need to get rid of him. It was the summer of '99. I was awakened from my sleep by a loud commotion. Daddy always told me never to come looking if I sensed trouble in the house. I didn't. I went to hide instead, lying flat on my back in the bathtub. Moments later there were gunshots. I closed my eyes and prayed to the heavens.

It was another thirty minutes before I left the tub and tiptoed down the stairs, peeking around corners. Whoever it had been was long gone. I made my way over to the living room, tears came streaming from my eyes. I was young but I lived in the hood and was no stranger to gunshot wounds. I picked up the phone, dialed 911, and told them my daddy had been shot. I ran over to see if he was okay. I was crying profusely. I could barely see when I knelt down beside him. "Never forget everything I taught you." Those were his last words.

"I love you, daddy. Don't leave me."

He smiled... and that was that.

When mama and the police finally arrived, daddy was long gone. Responses to calls for help from Godby were always slow.

Daddy never kept work in the house, but he was a known drug dealer. The authorities wrote his death off as drug-related. They didn't care. He was just one less nigga they had to worry

4

about. Mama and I moved into an apartment in Red Oak Projects that daddy had in case of an emergency. Big Rod would check up on us from time to time, but my uncle disappeared. No one told me where he went, and when I asked, they acted like it was a secret or something. Big Rod took me to get ice cream often after my daddy died. Every Friday I would wait anxiously in the window for him to show up in his money green El Dorado. He would get out standing tall, big and black, putting you in the mind of Bruce-Bruce. I was always happy to see him and ran out the door to greet him, jumping up and down knowing that I was about to receive something to my childish delight. Mama liked it, too. It gave her a break.

Big Rod would lift me up, spin me around and put me in the front seat. It was on one of these days while waiting in line for ice cream at a Dairy Queens in Riverdale that some tall, bald, dark skin guy wearing blue jeans, all white soulja Reebox and a Lakers Jersey approached Big Rod and asked about my uncle.

"Heard anything from ya boy Ron?"

Big Rod shook his head. "No, and you won't either. Nobody has. I'm starting to think he's dead."

"That would be best for him," the man scoffed. He started to walk off but noticed me, and paused.

I turned to look up at Big Rod, who stared back at the man expressionless. I looked back at the man, he looked up at Big Rod and shook his head.

"That's crazy," he said.

Without another word, he walked away. Five minutes later, we got our ice cream, left, and headed to Riverdale Park where Big Rod watched me play until the sun began to set.

Weeks turned into months and as the year went on, ice cream Fridays with Big Rod became less frequent, and before I knew it, he stopped showing up altogether. That's when things changed and I began to feel the weight of my reality.

———

Mama was one of the baddest bitches in the hood until she started fucking with that shit. And yes, I do mean crack. She had a bitch ass boyfriend named Darrel who was always watching me. At ten years old, I was ignorant of the lust in his eyes and he eventually violated me. I had just come home from school and mama wasn't there, so that bastard had his way with me. She must have been chasing the best high of her life because she didn't return for hours.

Darrel was sitting on the sofa watching *Leprechaun In The Hood* when he saw me. "Hey baby."

"What the fuck? I'm not your baby," I said.

I went to my room to change clothes. I could feel the vibe of someone watching me. I turned around to find it was Darrel's nasty ass. These mere events along with the fact that he used to beat my mama were the reasons I was filled with distaste and rage when it came to him. "Get away from my door!" I yelled.

He came in, closing the door behind him. "Making big demands for someone so little."

He reached for me. I tried to run but he slapped the shit out of me. The force from his strong hand sent me reeling to the floor. I was disoriented and seeing stars as he began removing the rest of my clothes. "Just take it and the pain will go away," he spoke through clenched teeth. I was scared and tears were abundantly rolling down my cheeks. "I've been wanting this for a long time," he said, pinning me down with a rough grunt.

I tried to fight back but he was stronger than me. Every time

I tried to buck on him taking off my clothes he would slap me. Eventually, he got me naked and jammed his dick inside me. He broke my hymen and tore my insides apart. It hurt so bad. I cried and screamed the whole time. Blood was everywhere.

There are some things you can't see happening to you until they do. That was the day I stopped believing in God. I was only in the fifth grade and he'd done nothing but make my life hell. I figured I couldn't be sent to hell if I was already there. I didn't tell mama. She was too *dickmitized*. Plus, he was the one bringing in what little food we did have, if that counts for anything. Thursdays and Fridays were his days off and he wanted me to be there. On the days I wasn't, he would beat me. This went on for a while until I was more than fed up with his shit.

I awoke to him arguing with mama one morning. It escalated and I came to her defense. "Get off my mama!" I was trying to pull him away from her. I never saw his hand. I felt it, it sent me flying to the wall. My mouth was bleeding and my ears were ringing.

"Leave my baby alone!" my mama screamed from the floor of our small living room.

He stomped her and told her to shut up. That's when I ran out of the living room and came back with Darrel's .38 special. With hot, angry tears pouring down my face, I screamed at the top of my lungs for him to get off my mama. He turned and looked me in the eyes.

"Shoot me, bitch, if you got the heart."

I thought about all the shit he did to me, and I pulled the trigger twice.

BWA! BWA!

His eyes were a mixture of shock and disbelief as he hit the floor, bleeding to death. The gun fell from my trembling hands.

1

Mama screamed like Tyra Banks in *Higher Learning*. I sat on the carpet and stared at Darrel's lifeless body. The nosy ass neighbors called the police and they took me away. I did ten months in the Metro RYDC.

Mama never came to see me, let alone claim me and I was eventually placed in a group home in the middle of Hillandale, another neighborhood in College Park with seven other girls. All of them were lame as hell, except one. Her name was Chelsea. I didn't know much about her because she never talked about her past. Still and yet, for some reason, I liked her in the type of way I should've liked boys. A lot of girls hated me because all the boys wanted me, but I wasn't even interested in them, to be honest. I was attracted to pretty girls. I dressed feminine but I had more nigga tendencies than the average girl should. I guess because of the way I grew up. At least that's what I came to believe.

———

Everybody had a mentor who brought them things, except me, and when they came to visit the group home, I'd be assed out every trip. For months, I used to cry myself to sleep until one day I decided something had to shake. Now in the seventh grade, niggas would try to fuck with me but I would never buy into it. I knew what niggas wanted, and it didn't turn me on. I was repulsed by the thought of a dick inside of me. Chelsea turned me on, though. We were basically joined at the hip. She turned out to be quite gorgeous. She was a redbone with a petite frame, cute face, like one of those Disney girls, with long brown hair to frame it.

Anyway, when I realized I didn't like boys, I tended to keep a lot of female company. To my surprise niggas started to hate on me, throwing salt on my name when they could. All but one, his name was Redd. He had a light brown skin tone. His dreads were to his neck and he stood about five-nine with a medium build. His grandparents were strong believers in the teachings of Marcus Garvey, and his parents were Rootical Rastafarians who believed in the holistic way of life. While they were full Jamaicans who came to the States in the '80s, Redd grew up on Gresham Road in East Atlanta. He was a Grady baby to the fullest.

His family had come to America on a banana boat, running from the Kingston authorities. Once here, they changed their last name to Hicks and started over. Arriving in the middle of the crack era, Redd's father, Jamaica Ray, learned the recipe and went to work. He put together a crew of thoroughbreds and painted the city red. At the height of his success with Jamaican novelty shops, a Caribbean Cuisine spot, and a club called Amadu's, Raphael Hicks was born. That was two years before my time.

By Redd's eleventh birthday so much attention had been drawn to Jamaica Ray. The Feds had an ongoing investigation and eventually seized everything he owned. Jamaica Ray was arrested and extradited to Jamaica where he would never see the light of day again. Redd's mother was taken into Federal custody for several murders, conspiracy, and drug trafficking charges. Guilty with no way to escape, the woman hung herself. She was found in her cell one morning during breakfast. Redd said she was believed to have been pregnant, but he wasn't sure. It was sad.

Subsequently, Redd was adopted by a money hungry couple who didn't care how long he stayed out, what he did or who he did it with. Redd lived a lawless life. He believed that, because he was from ATL, he was above the law. He didn't take shit from nobody and his reputation made a lot of people scared of him.

Redd and I started rocking with each other. We smoked so much damn weed he started calling me Kush, and the name stuck. My girlfriends would get mad because they thought I was fucking him, but that wasn't the case. We were just cool. We even had our own secret duck off, that only we knew about, down the street from Mary McLeod Bethune Elementary. We'd meet there whenever Redd had stolen something and wanted to show off, which was often.

My first lick was with him. I was pretty fucking nervous. Not because it was my first, but because it was a dope boy named Champ. He had pull all through the city. At the age of eighteen, he had more money than most niggas his age. I mean, he wasn't Big Meech or nothing but he damn sure was plugged in. Redd didn't seem to care, so I said fuck the shit too. His spot was on the eastside and I hardly went out that way.

We went in through the window of his ground level home in Meadow Lane off Glenwood Road. We found a .380, eight hundred dollars, and some weed. Redd said it was a Quarter Pound.

Although we didn't get much, Redd let me keep the .380. That was my first strap. The money and weed were split down the middle. Four hundred was the most I ever had in my pocket. Most of my money came from females I fucked with. I had a mouthpiece for a bitch because I knew what they wanted. Chelsea would get mad when she saw me with other girls. Couldn't say I blamed her, though. I was jealous at times myself. The only difference was I never showed it. I had a reputation to keep. I could have any bitch I wanted and the ones who got no talk were green with envy.

I was jumped more times than I care to remember. I stayed getting into fights and stayed thirsty to hit licks with Redd. He just seemed to know so much. I began to see him as my only way out the hood but he saw hitting licks as his only way out. Still, we were all we had.

CHAPTER TWO

MATTER OF TIME

I stopped going to school at thirteen. It wasn't cold turkey. I couldn't just drop out because of the rules of the group home plus the law required school until sixteen. So, I skipped nearly every day and went to fuck with Redd. He'd quit going not long after turning fifteen. There was no point in going to school for niggas like him, let him tell it. "You don't work, you don't eat. You don't grind. You don't shine," he sometimes said. "Nobody gives kids like us a chance, Kush. So, we have to take chances."

For me, school was just another place to meet new girls. I wasn't a stud. I dressed feminine. I even styled my long hair but that seemed to make boys like me even more. Daddy told me about boys once. He said most of them only wanted one thing. And a girl like me, every nigga wanted to fuck. I was caramel skin with long black hair and green eyes. Not much titties, but my ass made up for that though. People said I had one like Brooke Valentine. I was practically beating boys off with a stick.

My last day of school was the day everybody's shit from their locker went missing from the locker room while everyone was in PE. I had like twelve phones and two hundred dollars, but some scary ass bitch saw me and said she was going to tell so I pulled a knife on her and put it to her jugular. "Bitch don't get fucked up!" I said in the most menacing tone I could muster.

While I was sitting in my six-period class, the principal came and got me. When I got to the office, she was sitting there crying, and I already knew what it was. I was expelled and charged with terroristic threats and aggravated assault. After 30 days in Metro RYDC, I could no longer return to McNair Middle School. I started alternative school but there were no decent girls, so there was no point in going.

———

Chelsea skipped school one day to chill with me. When Redd and I picked her up off Sylvan Road she was shocked to see the bandage on the side of my neck. It was covering my first tattoo.

"Oh my God!" Chelsea exclaimed. "Let me see!"

I peeled the Band-Aid back and turned my neck to give her a better view. It was my name *Kush* surrounded by stars and music notes. Redd let us out at the Kroger on Flat Shoals.

"Aye Kush, get at me later."

We began our walk towards the group home. Across the street, they were building a Wal-Mart where Club 20 Grand used to be.

"I can't believe you actually went through with it," Chelsea said.

"I wasn't going to but Redd amped me up."

"You know the group home staff is going to be mad, right?

I shrugged then smiled. "Oh, well. It's a little too late for that now."

"Are you getting any more?"

"Hell yeah."

"Ooow, can I come with you?" Chelsea pleaded. "I wanna get tatted."

"Hmm, oh yeah? What you had in mind?" I asked.

A MARTA bus and several cars passed by after the light turned green up ahead.

"Weelll, I want some roses on my lower back and some butterflies coming across my back and my right shoulder," she said.

I couldn't help but picture her naked with the tattoos she said she wanted, in the areas she said she wanted them. It sounded good but I just knew she didn't know what she was getting herself into.

"You know all that's going to hurt, right?"

She didn't miss a beat. "So, you survived."

"Just saying. Don't say I didn't warn you."

"I'll live," she insisted.

We got to the group home and went around back to my window. I unlocked it before leaving this morning to meet Redd. No one was here but us. The other five girls were at school. Ain't no telling where the staff was. If they so happened to show face we'd just tell them we weren't feeling well so we left early. Either that or haul ass. Chelsea sat on my bed while I went to the closet to find some clothes to change into.

So what did you have in mind for your next tattoo?" she asked breaking the silence.

"I'ma get *Self* on my right eyelid, and *Made* on the other."

"Really?" Chelsea's ton. choked.

I turned just to see the look on her face and immediately bust out laughing. "No silly. I want to get *R.I.P Richard* on my side."

She looked somewhat relieved. "Oh, I was about to say."

"You couldn't have thought I was serious, could you?" I asked, picking out a pair of boy shorts and a tank top.

"I'm not surprised by a lot of things you do these days. You never cease to amaze me, Kush."

I took off my school shirt, sat on the bed in my bra and jeans, and removed my shoes. I looked to my right to find Chelsea staring at me. "What you lookin' at?" I asked extra girly like. She smiled and kissed me. I kissed her back and we started tonguing each other down. I was on fire. I was wet and my nipples were hard. At the same time, I was nervous. I had plenty of girl-friends, but I'd never actually had sex with any of them. I put my hand between her legs. She was just as wet. I thought she was going to resist but instead, she opened her legs up wider. I rubbed on her pussy and a soft moan escaped her lips. It drove me fucking crazy. I helped her remove her shirt and bra while kissing her neck and titties. I looked her in the eyes. She nodded and I kept going.

Panties off, I stared at her pussy, which was comforted by moist, silky hairs. So pretty, I couldn't wait to taste it. Easing her back on the bed, I spread her legs and sucked her toes while I played with her wet pussy. Then, slowly, I began kissing up her leg until I got to her pearl tongue. I was so turned on by the way she wined and moaned for me.

"Kush," she moaned as I aggressively started licking and tugging on her clit. She went crazy! "Damn, Kush, baby it feels so good."

Her pussy was so wet and tight, oh my goodness!

16

"Aghh, Kush," Chelsea cried out. "Please don't stop. I-aghh!" She wrapped her legs so tightly around my head and started bucking, as she came hard.

Her legs gave and she fought to stop trembling. I was mesmerized. Her shaking grew faint until it faded completely and she smiled down at me. She sat up, laid me on my back, and started to undress me. Once my clothes were off she started sucking my nipples.

"Chelsea," I moaned, as she eased her way down between my legs. I wrapped her hair around my hand as she worked that tongue of hers. It felt so good. Damn.

"Am I- do you like it?" she whispered.

The feeling was so euphoric I couldn't bring myself to respond. Then I came. Afterward, we cuddled up in the bed naked and just embraced the moment.

"Kush?" Chelsea asked.

"Huh?"

"Who's Richard?"

Her question caught me off guard. Then it hit me- the tattoo I wanted. "My daddy," I said.

"Oh." Chelsea paused; her eyes wandered. I could tell she was thinking. "Was he nice?"

"The nicest in the world," I said with a slight smirk.

She tilted her head to look at my face. "What about your mom?"

The question struck a nerve, and I tried not to show it. "Um... I mean shit... what about your parents?"

She looked away. "I really don't know."

"What you mean?"

"I never knew them. They gave me up when I was born."

I started to speak but stopped short. I know I probably

should have tried to comfort her with my words, but I didn't. I couldn't think of anything to say. Nothing would've helped or changed the way she felt. Having a fucked up past of my own, I knew at times it was best to stay silent. Talking about it only brought intense emotions and I wasn't in the mood for lending a shoulder to cry on. Not that I wasn't considerate. I just wasn't affectionate. I had become emotionally unattached in an attempt to block out my own pain.

After Chelsea, I started experimenting with other girls I'd been kicking it with, and recklessly so. Some guy named D'narius approached me one night at a party after it got back to him that I'd been pushing up on his girl. I was nearly dismissive when I told him that his girl wanted some of this good pussy.

"What the fuck you just said?" he shouted aiming his pistol in my face.

He had my complete attention now, and I could tell he was on the beans or something. He had a crazed look in his glazed eyes. I was no fool. One wrong move and it was over with. My palms began to sweat and out of nowhere a light skin guy with twists, who I'd never seen before, came up from behind and laid his hand on the dude's shoulder.

"Yo, D," he said. "You trippin', bra. That's a female."

D'narius hesitated but reluctantly put his pistol away and walked off. It wasn't until then that I realized I'd been holding my breath. Whoever that was with D'narius, looked like he wanted to start a conversation but he chose to walk away instead. This was probably best considering the current situation.

A few days later Redd pulled up on me in Shady Park whip-pin' a hot box. I told him about what happened. He was irate. "Get in," he said. We rode around looking for D'narius until we found him in Biscayne, off Old Nat, sitting on a green box. Just the sight of him made me angry.

"You got yo' strap?" Redd asked.

"Huh?" I knew I was trippin'.

The parking lot was fairly empty, but Redd rode like we didn't see him so we could ride to the back. He did this in every neighborhood before bussin' any type of move to be sure there were no blue boys present.

"Yo' .380. Is it on you?" Redd asked as he whipped around.

"No."

"It wasn't on you at the party either, was it?"

I was really trippin'. "No."

Redd shook his head and brought the car to a stop.

"Here," he handed me a chrome and black Colt .22 auto-matic. "Handle that."

Barefaced, I got out the car, crept up on D'narius, and put the pistol to his head, in the front of the apartments, in broad daylight. He was down bad.

"Hold up, bitch, what the fuck you got goin' on?"

"Give me all yo' shit, pussy nigga!" I demanded.

"Look, bitch, I ain't g- "

I clocked the nigga upside the head with the .22, lo and behold the nigga started crying.

"I ain't gone be too many more bitches either, fuck boy! Now. Give. Me. All. Yo' Shit!"

He emptied his pockets, his broke ass ain't had nothing but forty dollars and some bappy ass weed. I snatched it with my free hand and shoved his chump change in my pocket while keeping the gun trained on his head. I didn't realize the power of a pistol before, but I damn sure did now. I was geeked. No wonder Redd robbed for a living. It was too easy.

"You ain't so tough now are you?"

He didn't say anything. I spat in his face and kicked him as hard as I could. It felt so good to see his fear of me.

"Say you a bitch!" I demanded.

He gave me the *'man cut me some slack, you got what you wanted face,'* "Goddamn, I gave you what y– "

I kicked him again. "Say you a bitch!"

I could tell he was pissed and probably more so because I was female. Either I was really embarrassed about how I went out that night at the party, or it was just in my blood. I don't know. I do know I had no issue with bussing him in the mouth if the next words he spoke wasn't what I told him to say.

He dropped his head. "I'ma bitch," he said.

I laughed, ran back to the car and hopped in. We ducked off, and Redd told me he caught the whole thing on camera. It was a joke to me, but he showed me the video and I cried laughing. What I'd done was fucked up, but I still felt empowered by it. My first armed robbery and already I'd been turned out.

Redd suddenly turned serious. He pointed out that I was on another level and although that lick was chump change, he promised to one day put together a lick to set us straight for life. He made it clear that slippin' was a no-no. Especially for jackers.

"In our world," Redd said. "When you slip, you fall hard."

Everywhere I went from then on, I was strapped. If my guns couldn't go, neither could I. Redd put the video on *YouTube* and started telling everybody to check it out. At first, I felt like Cain in *Menace To Society* when O-Dog wouldn't stop showing the tape of the corner store robbery. Somewhere between the props and the street recognition I was given, stopped caring.

D'narius was hurt but he wasn't making any noise about it. Which was smart of him. Better to have holes in your ego than your body. In my eyes, he was just a weak ass nigga hopping on the X, thinking he's Superman. At my age, I didn't know everything, but I did know there would be no threats next time.

CHAPTER THREE

TRUE TO THE GAME

R edd was my ace. We did everything together. We kicked doors, robbed niggas, and we even sexed some of the same girls. There wasn't a soul in College Park we rocked with harder than each other. I was still green to some parts of the street life but whatever I was ignorant to, Redd was quick to fill me in on. He taught me a lot of shit. To his credit, not everything was negative, but rolling blunts, how to drive, and how to peel cars were most definitely in his curriculum. They were all, in my mind, things a girl needed to know when she was embracing the mentality of getting it how she lived. I was a fast learner. I got good at what I was taught. How to move in the streets was no different. After much practice, peeling cars had become one of my strong points. I never had to walk again.

By age sixteen I drove a different whip every day. All around the hood people began to notice. It became clear that I was about my money, and I was respected more because of it. I started boosting clothes from all the malls in the 678, 404, and 770 areas. I was networking so hard I never sat on anything. It was gone almost as quick as it came. You couldn't tell me I wasn't one of the baddest in the game. I took shit from no one. Big, tall, short, or small; I could care less.

I still stayed in the group home but I was never there. Chelsea started complaining about the amount of time we spent together. It wasn't enough for her. She'd swear up and down that, I loved the streets more than I loved her and I would swear that I didn't but sometimes I felt in my heart she was probably right. I was addicted to fast money and the lifestyle that came with it. The streets were my drug of choice and I stayed down for the high. I chased it with a passion, the same way mama chased that crack rock when I was younger.

All the girls who were originally at the group home when I arrived had turned eighteen and moved on with their lives. All except Chelsea. She and I had two more years left. Nothing changed, though. Just a whole new set of hatin' ass bitches. Honestly, it wasn't that niggas wanted to fuck with me, or that I always had something going on. It wasn't even because my closet was full of the flyest shit; Gucci, Fendi- you name it. It was the fact that they wanted to taste my pussy or they wanted me to taste theirs. But I couldn't go out like that. None of them were bad. Some of them were straight, but a bad bitch like me only fucked with bad bitches. It was a reputation thing.

My rep had grown so much that I found myself interacting with a lot of individuals. If I didn't know them, they had definitely heard of a bitch name Kush. A lot of niggas wanted to kill me and Redd, but they could get it in blood. That's how I felt, and I was quick to remind Redd every chance I got. He responded, "no one knew what they would do until they were placed in the situation." I took it as him doubting I was capable of pulling the trigger. I never bothered to remind him that my first body was at ten. He would come to know the truth, however.

————

I received a call from a pimp who wanted several thousand dollars in female designer clothes. In a stolen Power Ranger red Monte Carlo, I pulled up on him in The Summit Hotel's parking lot on Fulton Industrial. I whipped around back under a streetlight.

"This everything?" he asked after I popped the trunk to let him see what I had.

"Just about- what you was looking to get?"

He opened another bag and sifted through. "I mean, I like what you got but you can't shoot me no deal?"

I sucked my teeth.

"Nigga you got my money? We done talked numbers already."

"Yeah, I got you right here."

Something about the way he moved didn't sit right. I grew up with takers and I knew the signs. He was good, but it was all there. Before I could act on my observation, he was coming off the waist with a pistol.

"You know what it is, bitch. Come on with it!"

I put my hands up. "What? Look, you can have that shit."

He pushed me back.

"I know I can. What you thought it was, huh? A pimp pay a hoe?"

With the gun trained on me, he transferred all of my shit

from my trunk to the back seat of his car. All the while, I waited for him to slip. If it had been Redd and me, he would be lying face down naked with arms stretched out. He was either under-estimating me or he didn't know what the fuck he was doing. Regardless of which, he would pay. He put the last of the bags in the backseat.

"Now get up out of here before I bus' yo ass. And if I ever catch yo' ass trimmin' on the Westside again I'ma turn your lil ass out, understand me?"

I nodded, turned, took three steps, and glanced over my shoulder to find him opening his car door. I grabbed my .380 from the small of my back and fired four rounds. He pitched forward into the corner of the door. I ran up and put two in the back of his head. Hopping quick into the Monte Carlo, I peeled off.

I buried my pistol in some woods in Union City. I loved the gun, but with a body, it had to go. After the evidence was taken care of, I parked the Monte by our duck off spot in Hillandale and went back to the group home. It had been a long night, I had somewhere important to be in the morning.

———

I pulled up at the shop in Marietta in front of the tall ware-house gate. It's been a while since I spoke to Fuwah. I'd finally received the call I've been waiting on. The intercom buzzed, I identified myself and drove forward as the first of two gates opened. The second opened only after the first was secured, allowing me to pull into the chop shop. It was owned by an Arab named Ali Bahba but ran by his nephew Fuwah. Your average 'welcome to 7/11, my friend' type of Arab. Mid-height and balding. He was cool, but the money came before anything. We had met through the owner of the last shop I pulled jobs for, a Russian named Vlad who was a part of some group called the Underground Foreign Organization- UFO. Fuwah, who was also a member of this clandestine group, just so happened to visit Vlad's shop when I showed up with a cream-colored Benz that Redd and I hijacked from some guy the night before.

Vlad was once again trying to rip me off. We were going back and forth until Fuwah stepped in and asked me what I was looking to get for the Benz. Without another word, he pulled a wad of money from his pocket and gave me what I asked for. I could tell Vlad didn't like the play, but the fact that he didn't speak on it rang loud and clear that whoever Fuwah was, he was someone important. I smelled opportunity. So, despite the crumbs I was being fed to risk my freedom, I stayed down. In time, I was able to sidestep the middle-man and meet the plug when it turned out that Vlad had been undercutting Ali Bahba's weapon trade by secretly contacting his clientele, offering them the same deal at a lower price.

I showed up at Vlad's spot in a greenish-gray Chevy Camaro on Duces when I was told Vlad was no longer in business, but if I was still interested my service could be of use. I was with it. Later that day I pulled up to a Marietta address. Fuwah was who I was there to see.

"Oh, there she is!" A familiar voice snapped me back out of my reverie.

I shut the door and turned to find him standing behind me.

"Hey, Fuwah."

"Platinum Kush. How are you today?"

"I'm fine, and you?"

"Aah, I can't complain. You know what they say, though. Anything can happen between yesterday and tomorrow, eh?"

"True," I said above the drilling and wielding. "So, what's up? What's the move for today?"

Fuwah looked confused. "A thousand pardons?"

I laughed. "Let's get down to business."

"Why, yes," he gestured. "Right this way."

I followed him through the shop, from one garage to the next. Two Arabs struggled to put a door on a car that they'd removed from another, while two others worked to put a new fender in place. My attention was caught by a grand Rolls Royce between a silver Audi and a white Escalade. I was reminded of the wealth I wanted for myself. Fuwah paused near a tarp-covered car to one end of the garage. I couldn't wait to see what he had for me.

Fuwah snatched off the tarp. "This is your new car, Miss Platinum." He presented it like an Arabic deal or no deal prize announcer. I was shocked, and not in a good way either. I stood staring at the car like I couldn't figure out what it was. Disappointed didn't cut it. I heard of riding low-key, but damn, put a bitch in a Dodge Magnum or something. I could even go for a Chrysler 300, but a *fucking* KIA?

"Aw Fuwah, you shouldn't have," I gushed.

"Now Kush, no need to put on a show. Just hear me out."

I smiled like the cat that ate the canary.

"It has satellite radio, a police scanner, a hidden duck off spot where you can hide all the kush you want, and best of all, everything's the way you like it... new."

I walked around to the driver's side and got in.

"See?" Fuwah pointed. "Steering wheel, yes? Now look," he

touched a button on the dash and the panel slid up to reveal a seven-inch monitor in place of the airbag.

"Are you fucking serious, Fuwah? I feel like I'm on *Pimp My Ride* right now!"

"Who, my what?"

I adjusted my seat. "*Pimp My Ride*... you know, X to the Z-Xzibit?"

"Aah, I see, like a museum exhibit."

I gave up. "Never mind, it's not important."

Fuwah shrugged.

"I'm not completely against flashy things, as you can see. I am against drawing attention to yourself when you are already up to no good, yes. I have a daughter your age. The things you do, keep on the inside and the outside can only assume. You see, my friend?"

The keys were in the ignition, and I was ready to take my new car for a spin. I wasn't worried about anything. I'd been dealing with Fuwah long enough to know his whips were official. When ready for sale, each car went through a trial process to include several parking violations. Those that weren't towed, passed and were sold or- the case with the KIA -given as payment in place of money.

"'Thanks, Fuwah, you've really outdone yourself this time."

Fuwah handed me a business card through the window. "Don't mention it. Take this."

"What for?" I asked.

"My people at the DMV. Ask to speak to Yazha Qiya'am. You're already approved for your license. You must go take a photo, that's all. And be sure you go. You don't want to get arrested for driving without a license."

I put the card in my visor. "Will do, and thanks again Fuwah."

"Okey-dokey, no problem."

————

I was in and out of the DMV and was on my way back to College Park quicker than I thought. My phone rang. It was Chelsea again for the 50th time, I had to pick her up. At the Shell gas station on Old National and Pleasant Hill, I pulled into the unusually crowded lot, stopped at the pump, and went inside. I waited behind three people, checking the cashier out the whole time. She was a young Indian girl. Older than me but still young with a nice smile and shape. Her nametag read Krupa. I reached the counter, paid twenty dollars in gas, then pointed to the cigarettes behind her. "How much are those Newports shorts?"

"$5.36," she said with a heavy accent.

I shot her another ten and told her to keep the change, making a mental note to get to know her better in the near future. I was pumping gas and listening to the car beside me bump T-Pain's *Can't Believe It* when a silver Impala caught my attention as it came to a quick stop in the middle of the street. It made a U-turn then swerved into Shell's parking lot. On alert now, it hit me that my gun was in the duck off spot in the car. The Impala's passenger window slid down and a pistol was suddenly visible. My fight or flight senses kicked in and, unable to fight, I took flight.

BOOM! BOOM! BOOM!

Shots rang out as people screamed and ran for their lives. *These niggas trying to kill me,* I thought. No sooner was the thought completed, I felt a sting to my leg and I fell. Whoever shot me must've thought I was dead because they swerved off, leaving the gas station in pandemonium. "Somebody call the police!" I heard someone yell above the noise.

I finally get a *legit* whip and this bullshit jumps off. I ain't even get a chance to pull up at the group home. Them hating ass bitches would've been so fucking jealous. I was in excruciating pain. I couldn't help but cry. I thought I peed on myself until I looked down and saw red. So much fucking red. Whoever said getting shot didn't hurt, is a lying motherfucker! The crowd surrounding me was getting thick. I was sure I saw my daddy looking from afar before I passed out.

————

I was in and out of consciousness. Ventilators and breathing machines were set up. They drew blood to test, gave blood to stabilize, and did X-rays to find out where the bullet had pierced me. I regained full consciousness and discovered my leg in a cast and elevated. I looked to my right to find Chelsea beside me sleep in a chair. She looked so peaceful. Still dazed from painkillers, I admired her beauty. As if on cue, her eyes fluttered. "Good morning," she said with a half-hearted smile.

"Hey," I said. "Where am I?"

She blinked a couple of times and sat up facing me. "Grady Memorial Hospital."

"How long have I been out?"

"A couple of days. I was starting to think the doctor gave you too much morphine."

I looked at the ceiling sling. "So, what did they say about my leg?"

"It's fine, you just have to stay off of it for a while. The bullet broke a bone, but other than that and the hole it left, you have nothing to worry about. You've already been seen by a trauma surgeon and a pulmonary physician. So, you don't have to take my word for it."

"I believe you."

She stretched, then got up and leaned on my bed beside me.

"Well, that's good to know. Besides, they just left after giving you a tetanus shot and more antibiotics less than ten minutes ago. Really hate to bother them after all the hell I put them through these last couple of days."

That put a smile on my face. "Oh really, now?"

"Yep, World War III. I even convinced the group home staff to let me stay here with you until you are better. I don't trust doctors. Especially ones with a license to use anesthetics. I watch Lifetime. I know what's goin' on."

I laughed. "Has anyone ever told you, you watch too much TV?"

"Has anyone ever told you, you run the streets too much?" she shot back.

I was annoyed. Partly because she was right, and because she was acting like she was my mama, which reminded me of the fact that I didn't have one.

One thing I'd learned over the years dealing with so many faces, was that truth was expressed through jokes. I knew this was coming. I knew it just as sure as I knew she was right. But the lifestyle I became accustomed to wasn't going to support itself. I loved Chelsea, but I wasn't about to be walking around broke for nobody. So, what if I run the streets? I have goals, and accomplishing them is all that mattered. Hell, I was doing this for her, too. Other than getting shot, everything was right on track. Someday she would thank me. Either that or bury me.

"Why'd you get so quiet all of a sudden?" she asked.

"Come on Chelsea, at least wait until I'm discharged from the hospital to give me the Coretta Scott King speech. I just woke up, damn!"

It came out a lot harsher than I intended, but I was frustrated. Not being able to walk. Lord knows I was tired of this conversation. Mostly because she made valid points that I couldn't dispute without making me look stupid. I swear she should be a politician. At least then she'd be getting paid to be someone's migraine. I laid back and stared at the ceiling. Her expression went from flabbergasted to angry in seconds.

"Well excuse me for not noticing you were sleep while I cried my eyes out, sitting beside you in an uncomfortable position for the last couple of days. But what difference would it make if I waited or not? Whether we talk here or on the moon, you'd still try to find a way to drown me out. Do you even know who shot you?"

My head immediately snapped in her direction. "I damn sure do. And as soon as my leg heals, they'll be keeping Darrell company. Trust and believe that! This shit ain't over with. Not until I'm the last bitch standing."

Chelsea stood there staring in disbelief. I blew my top this time. She had struck some serious nerves. It wasn't like she was telling me anything wrong. She never did, and despite the fact I never listen, she was still there for me whenever I needed her. I felt like shit. She didn't deserve that. I owed her an apology. The most sincere apology I could muster.

I worked up the nerve just as two detectives dressed in button downs and slacks walked in. If it wasn't for the badge on their waistline, I wouldn't have noticed they were detectives at all. They looked more like white Jehovah Witnesses. One was young, the other was older. The younger one was average height, medium build with brown hair. The older guy was somewhat short and stout with the salt and pepper thing going on. I had no kick it for either of them.

"Excuse me Miss," the younger one addressed Chelsea. "Could you step outside while we have a word with your friend?"

Chelsea looked at me. She knew I couldn't stand cops. Her eyes told me she'd stay if I wanted her to. I hated that shit. The effect it had on me caused my emotions to swell and I wasn't fond of that emotional stuff. I needed a reprieve from her presence. I nodded. Chelsea left, closing the door behind her.

The young detective spoke first. "I'm Detective Cunningham and this is my partner Detective Ross. We just have a couple of questions concerning the incident that took place at the Shell gas station. That way we can follow up on any leads and possibly catch the cowards that did this to you." Cunningham pulled out a small pad and a pen, while his partner stood idly by. He flipped to a blank page and continued. "So, how did you get to the station?"

"I walked."

Cunningham's brows rose. "That's odd. The cashier said you bought some gas. Know anything about the KIA found at the pump?"

I didn't miss a beat. "Nope."

Cunningham eyed me like I shot myself.

"Well, that would be even stranger because your fingerprints are inside."

I was beginning to get frustrated.

"Am I a victim or a suspect?"

"Listen kid, don't bullshit us," Ross spoke up. "We're trying to help you but you have to help us. The only reason you're not cuffed to that bed right now is because we have daughters your age.

"Whatever."

Cunningham and Ross glanced at each other. Cunningham decided to give it another shot.

"Do you have any beef with anyone? Anyone you can think of? Just give us a name, something to start with."

I looked him dead in the eyes. "Nobody."

I honestly didn't know who shot me. I had too many enemies. One thing I did know is that the streets talk.

———

I spent the next couple of months on bed rest at the group home. Chelsea took care of me and nursed me back to health. I hated being in the house with a bunch of drama queens, arguing, gossiping, and swearing up and down they were strictly-dickly but secretly telling me they want to taste me.

Redd was mad when he found out about my ordeal at the gas station. He spazzed on me like I was the suspect.

"What I tell you 'bout getting caught slippin'?"

"My bad. I was just finna go get some pussy. Didn't think I needed a pistol for that. Wasn't like I was naked. I put it in my duck off spot in the car."

Redd treated me like a nigga. Sometimes it was okay, and other times it wasn't cool at all.

"Kush, the street don't give a fuck about you! We got too much going on right now to be taking losses and casualties.

Focus. You gotta stay ten toes down and ten steps ahead of the bullshit!"

It hit me then. My daddy had once told me something similar. Then I thought back to the night I got shot, how he'd been at the scene. He'd saved me. I could feel him there with me. I cried later. Not because I got caught slipping. I just miss my daddy so much.

———

After slowly recovering, I got on my trap girl shit. Redd hit a lick for a couple pounds of gas with some new nigga on the block name Polo he'd been running with. The same nigga who had told D'narius to fall back when he pulled the pistol on me that night at the party. Small world.

Just about all the girls smoked, so I sold a good little bit my first day. Most of us got checks, so whatever the group home didn't spend, we kept the scraps. That two for fifteen had me bumpin', too. I was really cappin' on the low because both sacks were .4, which meant I was booming .8 for the fifteen. Not even a whole gram. They tried to tell me I couldn't do this shit, and I had to prove them wrong. Niggas probably didn't think I knew how to sell for real, thinking they were getting over when I was the one getting it in. The trap, I learned, was in my blood. Something I was good at but wasn't so enthusiastic about. I was with the stickup gig. It was too easy. So easy that Redd believed it was our only way out the hood.

A girl name Meeka was sitting on my bed when I came home one day. *This bitch done lost her mind,* I thought. *In my room, on my bed. Oh, she finna get it.*

She looked up. "Kush, what's really good?"

"Da fuck you talkin' bout?" I snapped.

"I'ma keep it a-hunnid. I wanna taste yo' pussy."

I looked at Meeka. Dark skin, short, thick as fuck with short hair like Nia Long. I was thrown by how straightforward she was. Everyone knew me and Chelsea had something going on. Meeka was cute, and I'd thought about her being on my level. I was turned on for some reason, and at the moment I wanted her to taste me just as bad as she said she wanted to.

"What you expect to get from this?" I asked. "I hope you don't want me to return the favor cause that's out of the question."

She smiled and got up on me. I took a step back in an attempt to get my mind right, but she backed me in a corner and grabbed my ass.

"Nothing," she whispered in my ear.

I licked my lips, horny as hell. I wanted... no, needed this. She kissed me and went to shut the door. When she came back she undressed me and told me to get on all fours with my ass in the air. I did as she said, and she got behind me and went to eating my pussy so, so, sooo good.

"Damn," I arched my back, encouraging her to clean her plate.

I wanted to feel her tongue deeper inside me. I believe she was giving me the best head I'd ever had in my life.

"Say my name," she said.

"Meeka,"

"Say it louder!" she said as her tongue stroked my clit.

"Oh, shit, Meeka!" I screamed.

I couldn't believe the bitch had me saying her name, but she was putting it on me. She licked and licked and it felt so good. She started going faster and faster. I was moaning like no one else was home. So loud, and I didn't give two fucks. She inserted two fingers in my pussy, moving them in and out. It drove me insane. I was beginning to cum when someone burst into the room.

"You bitch!" Chelsea screamed, pushing Meeka away from me. "Get off of her!"

Chelsea was staring at me with tears pouring down her face. "How could you?"

I was stuck. I couldn't say anything. In my loss for words, she slapped the shit out of me and ran out of the room.

"Chelsea, wait. I can explain!"

She was gone.

"Fuck her," Meeka said. "Let's finish what we started." She stuck her fingers all off in her pussy.

I psyched out. "Bitch, you ain't shit! You just got some good ass head. I used you for a nut and nothing more. Now leave me alone!"

She looked sick, but I could care less. Fuck her. I went to the bathroom to wash up. I grabbed some clothes and got dressed to go find Chelsea. As I walked, I started crying. I realized I loved Chelsea.

She was in Flat Shoals Park with a group of niggas I didn't pay much attention to when I caught up to her. "Chelsea, I'm sorry. Can we please talk?"

"No."

I walked closer to her, still ignoring the seven niggas surrounding her.

"I like them green eyes," one of them said.

"Damn, she got a phat ass," another stated ignorantly.

In my feelings, I lost it again. "Fuck y'all thirsty ass niggas!" I turned back to Chelsea. "Listen, I- "

One of the niggas hit me with a mean ass blindside, sending me to the pavement. The next thing I knew, all seven had pounced and my shit was getting stomped in.

"Yea, bitch, we told you we was gonna get yo' ass. Tell Redd his ass next!"

So worried about Chelsea, I didn't realize these were niggas I had beef with. Love does blind. All I could do was look at Chelsea. She was watching me get beat. Literally just standing there. I was suddenly aware that she'd set me up. Redd had told me that I was born by myself and I would die by myself. I'd forgotten once again and was caught down bad. Fuck love and fuck Chelsea! I returned to the group home looking like Rocky in the final round against Drago.

I waited all night for Chelsea, but she never came back. There was no telling what I would've done if she did. The last thing I wanted to do was call Redd and get cussed out about getting caught slipping again. I honestly didn't feel like hearing that shit. I had a serious headache. I laid down in my bed, mad as hell. I didn't want any staff to see me either. The first thing they would assume was I was getting beat on by some nigga like the rest of these low-class hoes. Yeah, right.

CHAPTER FOUR

MOUTH DUCK TAPED

It's been a week since I got jumped and my face had finally cleared up. Chelsea never came back so they put a warrant out for her arrest. Sometimes I wonder where she is, then I see the scars on my face in the mirror and say fuck her all over again. Redd found out about me getting jumped. I swear he knows everything. It wasn't a pleasant conversation.

Girls at the home called themselves having attitudes. They knew what went on between me and Meeka, thanks to her and that shit Chelsea pulled. I was baffled they seem to think I gave a fuck. They knew better than to say anything smart. I was more than ready to beat a bitch ass.

———

I heard some noise one night but ignored it until I heard footsteps outside my door. I took the cover off my head and there stood four police officers pointing pistols at me.

"Don't move!" They yelled.

I was scared so I didn't. They threw ghetto bracelets on me and read me my rights.

"What did I do?" I asked.

"Armed Robbery."

My heart stopped. Damn. As they took me to the squad car, all the girls kept asking, "Kush, what you do?" as if they couldn't see the police. Dumb ass hoes. They nosy assess ain't care anyway. They just wanted to fuck with a high-class bitch like me. I saw Meeka as they drug me out. She had a sneer on her face as if she was glad I'd finally gotten what I deserved.

After being placed in the all-white College Park Police Department squad car, they took me to the interrogation room at a precinct. They told me they'd be back in a minute but I watch too much First 48 so I figured it would be a while. There was no way in hell I would incriminate myself. I'd robbed a lot of niggas. I sat down and tried to think of which one they might have on me.

I sat for forty-five minutes before the detectives showed face, and I'll be a fuck nigga's bitch if it wasn't Cunningham and Ross. The same detectives who worked the case when I got shot at the Shell gas station. Both had manila envelopes in hand. I smelled Vendetta.

In the interrogation room was nothing but a fitting yet ominous small table which I was sitting at. Cunningham took a seat directly across from me while Ross, not surprisingly, chose to stand.

"Tell me about the robbery of Daisha Hunter," Cunningham asked, getting right to the point.

Daisha was some twenty-six-year-old chick Redd used to talk to from Washington Road. We got her for her Charger and six hundred dollars. Frivolous. At the same time, see no evil, hear no evil, and speak no evil.

"I don't know what you talking about."

Ross exploded. "That's how you want to play it? Okay! We got Raphael Hicks in the other room saying you did it. Now here's the thing, whether you go to jail or he goes, this case gets solved. So it doesn't really make a difference to me either way. However, if you'd like to walk away without spending the best years of your life rotting in a cell, I'd suggest you tell us what we want to know. You got that?"

They took me for some dumb bitch that didn't know the law or their tactics. That good cop, bad cop shit was played out. So was the turn them against each other, mind game.

I smiled. "I have absolutely no idea what you're talking about... whatsoever."

Ross slammed his fist on the table like that was supposed to scare me.

"You're gonna go down for ten years while Redd stays on the streets living good? What type of so-called boyfriend tucks his tail while his girl takes the fall?! You're supposed to be the one living it up. You're too pretty to get caught up in Redd's shit, dammit!"

Ten years was a long time. So long that I totally disregarded Ross's comment about Redd being my boyfriend. Yet, I couldn't go out like that. I looked them both in their eyes.

"Fine," Cunningham said. "Let her get the time. She doesn't care. Another young black woman, I guess. Believe me when I say we're going to get Redd. And when we do, you'll both be in prison."

Cunningham got up and they made their way to the door. Then Ross stopped and faced me. "I'm going to make sure you get ten years. Even if I have to stay and work this case all day and night, Ms. Love. It's over with for Kush." He slammed the door.

They took me to Metro RYDC, did my intake, and took me straight to the room. Redd didn't get locked up, lack of evidence. They had my fingerprints. It was 3:15 am when I hit the mat, and it seemed as though only minutes had passed before I felt someone tapping me. I moved the covers from over my head to find a female who was obviously my roommate, bending down over me. She was light skin, 5'10 with micro braids. She couldn't have weighed more than 145lbs, soaking wet. She had c-cup titties and a voluptuous ass to go with them.

"You going to breakfast?"

With no words, I got up to make my bed. This wasn't my first rodeo. She took the hint and left the room.

I got myself together and came out, entering the day room. All the other females were lined up and ready to go. We wore blue jeans and gray T-shirts. I was in B-4, one of the only two female dorms in Metro. "Let's go Ladies!" Ms. Johnson yelled. She was the Juvenile Correction Officer on our unit. JCO's are what we called them. When the last females were out their rooms, we filed out of the dorm and headed to the chow hall. I took a deep breath and exhaled.

"Here we go again."

———

Days turned into weeks and weeks turned into months. Before I knew it, I had been locked up for nine months. Redd wrote me letters on the regular, but he wasn't old enough to come see me. He was too hot anyway. I'd told him to keep his nose clean and stay off the radar and, surprisingly, he did. He hadn't been locked up so far, and I was happy for him. I miss him so much. I needed him to make me laugh. He kept me tuned in to what was going on in the streets. A lot of throwback females I used to mess with back in the day wrote me also. I never wrote them back though. It didn't surprise me how juvenile wasn't too much different from the group home. Girls wanted to fuck and the rest hated me because all the niggas on the boys' side wanted to holla. I lost count of how many of them left letters in my folders in the education building.

A big, ugly butch-dyke lookin' bitch tried to talk to me. I had to put that hoe in her place. "Bitch! You betta get yo' Beanie Sigel lookin' ass out of my face!" I yelled. She was black as fuck, her hair was nappy, and her breath stank. She sat there looking stupid as the entire dayroom erupted in laughter. Even Ms. Johnson and Ms. C had to stifle their laughs.

Later that day I was walking by the shower when suddenly, without warning she threw me in a chokehold from behind, snatching me inside. "I heard you liked getting yo' pussy ate," she said. "I can do that for you. I want you so bad. I won't tell nobody." Her raspy whisper made my skin crawl.

"Nobody?" I asked, playing along.

"Not a soul."

"Okay," I said trying my best to sound both timid and convincing.

I was definitely waving the white flag, but at that point, I would've agreed to stick my tongue in her ass with no hands to get her musty arms from around my neck. It worked. She let me go, thinking that I would go to her room after lunch. This bitch was on some real fake, big dawg shit. Fuck she thought this was, high max? I was down bad. I knew I couldn't beat her head up.

To make matters worse, lunchtime was less than an hour away and I had nothing to even the odds. Too bad it ain't no pistols behind these walls. Still, though. I could never allow myself to be raped again. As long as there was life left in my body, I refused. I had to think of something fast.

As with anyone who lacked preparation, time seemed to work against me and before I knew it, B-4 was in line headed to the dining hall for lunch. Fuck the bullshit, my ass was at the end of the line where I could see the big brolly bitch. Peripheral vision wasn't good enough for me. I watched her grab her tray from the window and take her seat at the table with three other girls. Their stomachs were clearly made of steel. To eat at a table with someone so disgusting without immediately throwing up, should qualify you for some daring game show. I'd put my money behind either one of them on the next episode of *Fear Factor*.

She winked at me and smiled. I looked away with disgust in my heart and acted as if I didn't see her. She didn't know it, but that provocative shit pulled the last straw. This bitch had really lost her mind. I was officially losing my understanding. I finally made it to the window to grab my tray and on the way to my seat.

WHAM!

I slapped the shit out of her ass with the tray. She toppled over out of her seat and I was all over her. Relentlessly. I dropped bombs on her head with my tray as if my life depended on it. The girls who had been dining with her moments before took cover. By the time JCO's broke it up, her right eye was swollen and her nose was oozing blood. She had peanut butter and coleslaw mangled in her nappy ass head. She was a fucking mess.

"Let me go!" I snapped. "That bitch trying me!"

"It's over, Love. Calm down," Ms. Johnson said while attempting to restrain me.

"Ima kill that bitch. Get the fuck off me!"

"10-10! 10-10!" Ms. C yelled into her radio. "10-10 in the dining hall!"

"Love!" Ms. Johnson yelled. "It's done. You won, now calm down before assistance arrive and we have to use force!"

"Fuck that! Ima kill that bitch! Ima kill that bitch!"

BOOM!

The dining hall door burst open as a team of JCO's rushed in to assist Ms. Johnson and Ms. C in diffusing the altercation.

"Cuff up! Cuff up!" They yelled in unison as they wrestled me to the ground.

"Get off me! I screamed defiantly. "Let me go!"

No matter how psyched out I may have thought I was, at the end of the day, I was no match for a team of grown ass JCO's using Physical Control Measure techniques. I was cuffed and hauled to medical as the remaining juveniles enjoyed real live action at my expense. I'd done what none of them had the guts to do, which was put their foot down. Scary ass hoes. Fuck 'em and the JCO's too, with they fake DJJ Polo shirts and them ashy ass khakis. After a nurse looked me over, I was taken back to the dorm where I'd be placed on Pre-Hearing Confinement for the next 72 hours.

After being allowed to take a shower that night, I returned to my cell and the Control Room officer hit the light. I dried off then laid back on my uneasy cot in the dark, staring at the ceiling. These were the worst moments. In which I could imagine God up high getting a real kick out of how fucked up my life is. Adding insult to injury, he set aside these special moments where there was nowhere to run, nothing to do to distract me, and no sign of the sandman. All there was to do is think about my life. I've lived a nightmare ever since I was able to hold a memory.

I rubbed the scar the bullet left in my leg. It amazed me how vividly I could still feel the sting whenever I replayed the whole incident. My mind was a motherfucker. It had a real habit of locking in painful memories. I'd been shot with a .38 special. By who, though? I was sure I'd never know. A happy memory came to mind only to be chased off by treachery. Big Rod, followed by the realization of the empty promises he'd made. I pulled the cover over my head and faced the wall. My thoughts drifted to Krupa and how I'd never gotten the chance to get to know her on an intimate level. I thought of Fuwah and how spooked he must be by my disappearance. He probably knew where I was, though. He could find out just about anything he felt he needed to know.

I thought of all the niggas I'd robbed, all the random and premeditated faces of victims I'd shot. I thought about D'narius, my first stick-up victim. He's probably the one who shot me, with his pussy ass. I doubt it. But if so, then hats off to him for finding some nuts.

I was a little paranoid. I had to pay for all the wrong I did eventually, right? With my luck, I'd pay sooner rather than later. I'll take all my enemies with me to hell in the process. The thought marinated. I dozed off thinking about that night seven years ago, the night my whole life had flipped upside down. The point which set life on a permanent path of destruction. The night of my daddy's murder.

"Love. Love. Wake up," I heard a subtle voice say from afar, or so it seemed. I blinked my world back in focus to find Ms. Johnson in my room trying to wake me. I sat up on my cot.

"Why- what's going on?" I asked groggily.

"Well, nothing, actually. I was just letting you know that you're off of lockdown. I just need to make my last rounds with the detox wand and your seventy-two hours are up."

I laid back down and pulled the covers over my head. "Yay me," I said without interest.

When I didn't hear her exiting, I pulled the covers back from over my head. She stood there looking down on me, and for the first time, I realized that we were about the same height. She was a small woman; soft sandy skin with nice full lips and dark brown eyes. Her hair was in a ponytail as it was required to be by the rules, but she was good looking for an older woman. I could tell she was very pretty in her younger years. I wasn't one to converse with officers, but from what I could see, she seemed fair. As if she would help you in any way. At the end of the day, she was still the police. I couldn't see past the badge.

"What?" I said growing frustrated.

She had already woke me up out my sleep. I could've been dreaming about free-world shit. I could care less about being off lockdown. As long as the clock kept ticking, they could put me on long-term confinement for all I cared.

"You holding up alright in here?" she said.

The way she asked, it sounded like she was asking about something else entirely. I know when people have ulterior motives. I wasn't Ms. Cleo by far, but I had a feeling this visit was bigger than my time served on lockdown.

"What's that supposed to mean?"

She smiled. "I see you have a spirit of discernment."

"I don't know nothing about no spirits but I can smell bull-shit from a mile away. *MA'AM*."

"I see."

I sat up. "You see what?"

"You have a lot more sense than you let on."

"Okay wait, hold up. Here you go, you're doing it again."

"Doing what?"

"You keep on swinging double edge swords. Was that an insult or a compliment? Cause it could've been either or."

"There's no need to be so defensive, Love. I didn't come in here to down you, nor do I judge. Judging is for God, but if one must judge, let them judge themselves. The Bible says, *Let ye who is without sin cast the first stone*. You see me now but you don't know where I've been. I'm far from perfect, Love."

"Yeah," I shot back. "I didn't ask for your life story either, so what's your point?"

She smiled. "You most certainly did not, did you?"

The question sounded rhetorical so I didn't respond. I didn't know if she was trying to pick my brain or what, but it was kind of hard to be mean to someone who only responded with kindness. I decided to let her say what she had to say so she could go on about her business.

"Mind if I have a seat?" she asked, pointing at the end of my mat.

"Go ahead," I said, moving my feet out of her way and placing them on the floor. "Knock yourself out."

She sat down. "Do you believe in God?"

"Do you?'"

"Of course, I do. I've been through too much not to."

"So have I, but nothing's changed."

"How do you know?"

50

"Because it's my life. I'm the one living it!"

"Just because you don't see anything happening, doesn't mean that God isn't working on your behalf. Have faith and trust in God. He has you when no one does."

I stood up and paced my five-by-nine cell. Muffled noise from the dayroom drifted in. The door was pulled to but wasn't locked.

"How can you say that? There was a time when I prayed so much for a change in fortune, you would've mistaken me for a devoted Roman Catholic. Faith of a mustard seed my ass! If I get on my knees and pray I have to believe something. Since I was nine my life has been hell. I was only a little girl. What did I do to deserve the things I've been through? Better yet, why doesn't he answer if he's so real, huh? Tell me that!" I turned to faced her while I fought back tears.

I wouldn't let her see me cry. She looked at me with the most gentle expression.

"Believe it or not, sometimes God's greatest gift are unanswered prayers. It might not make much sense now, but someday it'll sink in. All I can say is the Lord works in mysterious ways. A lot of times people miss the Silver Lining because they're expecting gold. Don't try to understand God's logic, Love. It's beyond your reasoning. Don't shun him either. You have to tune in. Heed the signs of God the first time. Who knows if he'll warn you twice. Do you have a Bible?"

I stared at the floor. "No."

"Well do you want one?"

"'Look, I'm through wasting my time with things I can't see, Ms. Johnson. I tried to live righteously and I ain't feeling the lifestyle."

"Well, you can't shack up with the devil and expect God to

pay the rent, Love. Don't be deceived, God cannot be mocked. People reap what they sow. That's Life."

"No!" I yelled, caught in my feelings again. "What's life is the shit people from the hood face every day! No food, no help, no one who cares, hand me downs, that's life! In my world, sometimes you have to do the wrong thing to make shit right!"

Ms. Johnson stepped close to me. "And the wrong thing you did got you here in a cell. This is the result. You call this right? I'm not buying that, not from you, I'm not. Those aren't self-made thoughts that you speak. You're smarter than that and you and I both know it. Love, if you don't design your life, your life will be the result of someone else's design without your best interests in mind."

I took a step back. "So now I'm a follower? Is that what you're trying to say? Say it, Ms. Judging Is For God."

Ms. Johnson closed the gap between us, placing a hand on my shoulder.

"Love, I'm not judging you. All I'm saying is the results we have in our lives are based on the decisions we've made in the past. Therefore, your future will be the result of the decisions you make today."

I pulled away from her embrace. "You're right, I'll think for myself. Starting now. With all due respect, Ms. Johnson, I don't know you from a can of paint. My loyalty is to the ones I came up with. You're a JCO, police. You represent everything set up to keep people like me oppressed. In so many words, you're my enemy."

Ms. C was passing out snacks in the day room. The sound and commotion could be heard from here. Ms. Johnson look defeated.

"I'm sorry you feel that way, Love. I really am. I won't take up any more of your time. If you change your mind about coming out. Just call for me. I'll be in the day room."

There was a part of me that wanted to stop her as she turned to leave. A side of me that felt that she meant well. Never in my life had anyone spoke to me on the level she had. She was too late, though. I was stuck in my ways. She paused outside my door.

"You know what the saddest thing about betrayal is?"

I looked up at her.

"It never comes from your enemies." She closed the door softly.

CHAPTER FIVE

TURNING THE TABLES

They moved the butch-dyke to B-3. I found out her name was Tunk. She's from College Park Projects. Turns out she had nothing but a petty shoplifting charge. As if someone wouldn't notice her ugly ass trying to steal some fly shit. Imagine that, I just knew that bitch was J'd out on the streets.

I finally came out the room, all the bitches were on my bra strap. "I like your hair, you got some pretty eyes or what you mixed with?" Like I couldn't just be black and proud. I had no kick-it for these hoes. I was too focused on all the time the state was trying to give me.

This by far has been the craziest bid I'd ever done. I've been gone all this time and the deal remains the same; ten do seven! They got me fucked up. I'm too pretty to spend seven years with these ratchet ass bitches. I started plotting my escape. In the process, I learned how to manipulate. There were a lot of females who looked up to me and a lot more scared of me, so I didn't have to get my hands dirty. I had a roommate named Keisha who would beat a hoe ass. She was raw as hell. She got locked up for family violence. Keisha was cool as hell and pretty, too. Still, I never tried her. I didn't want to.

Time passed and I was coming up on seventeen. I was supposed to have gone to the county but my case was dropped from Superior to Juvenile Court a week before. That meant no more seven years. My attorney told me the worst-case scenario would be five at YDC. I wasn't trying to do that either. They really didn't have any evidence against me.

The day of my birthday just so happened to fall on a visitation weekend. Keisha had visitation, and I was sitting in the dayroom when she returned.

"We stupid straight," she said enthusiastically.

I could tell she was amped about something. "What you talking 'bout?"

"Why you ain't tell me?"

"Tell you what?"

She looked around the day room for possible eavesdroppers. "Come to the room."

We told Ms. Johnson to pop our door, then we locked down. That's when Keisha pulled out a fat bomb of weed and a lighter. I hadn't smoked in damn near a year.

"How'd you get it in?" I asked.

"My brother brought it to me. His partna gave it to him for me to give to you.

I spoke to Redd two days ago, he told me he had a birthday present for me. I wasted no time rolling the weed in tissue paper. It was kush. Redd had really shown his ass on this one. We rolled nine joints and sat on the bed. I covered the window and we blew it down. I was so high, I couldn't feel my toes. I looked at Keisha. She was laid back on her boat looking retarded. I busted out laughing, she started right behind me. I wanted to say something but I couldn't stop laughing long enough to get my words out. I made up my mind that night that I was going to get my ass home no matter what. It was something that I had to do.

Keisha went home and it didn't take long after for me to realize I'd made a real friend. Despite her freedom, our bond remained intact, if not stronger. She would write me frequently. She was a real live wire. A real rider, too. A lot of females who made friends with other girls would get out and ride for a couple months at the most, but as the months went by, Keisha stayed down. Almost a year had gone by and she was still riding. I've officially been locked up twenty-three months now. Too damn long. Court was coming in three weeks. It wasn't looking good on my end but I was ready to get it over with.

They were still mad that I wouldn't snitch on Redd. That's who they really wanted, and I was the only one who could give enough evidence to influence the judge to sign off on an arrest warrant. Wasn't happening. Redd still wrote me from time to time. He'd let me know that he missed me and that he was out there stuntin' and fuckin' bad bitches for me every day. That's what kept me going and stopped me from breaking down. He said he would come get me whenever I was ready to get the hell on. I told him to chill and I'd be fine. Honestly, I felt like he was doing enough, obligation wise.

Other girls in my shoes had flipped after being left high and dry by the niggas they called themselves being loyal to. The niggas had the nerve to get mad when all they had to do was keep it real the way their girl had kept it. That was one thing that made me and Redd so close. Loyalty. It was as if we had the same upbringing sometimes.

I continued to receive letters from former lovers, despite my stiff correspondence. I had yet to respond to a single letter. All this time had gone and I hadn't fucked around once. It hasn't been easy. What kept me celibate was the nurses' HIV/AIDS stats. They said one out of every ten girls incarcerated were infected. That was enough to hit home but lately, I've been getting wet from the subtlest hint at anything sexual. Most girls would wait for male officers to come by so they could finger themselves while they watched. For a girl like me whose only interest was in females, aside from my imagination or sex with the more than likely infected, I had no outlet. My libido was through the roof.

My roommate tested the waters. A short, thick, high yellow chick from Summer Hill. Her name was Erica. The tugging on her brain from rocking her braids too tight may have been the boost behind her attempt. Though most girls knew I messed around, they never tried me. We were on lockdown and Erica was kickin' what I called that *Haygood Flava*. She asked do I ever get horny.

"Of course, I do." Even the thought of where the conversation was headed was making me wet.

"Well, what do you do?" she asked.

"I play with myself."

"I'm tired of that, though," she wined. "Aren't you?"

I couldn't take it anymore. "You know I am. The question is what are we gonna do about it?"

She looked at me and smiled. "Damn, you sexy."

She said it low and enticingly. I was so turned on. I thought my nipples were gonna explode. From left field, the sound of the key lock shook us out of our erotic thoughts. The door swung open and it was none other than the heavyset brown skin woman I'd come to love, Ms. C.

"Jenkins," she said. "Pack it up."

"I'm going home?" Erica asked with a mixture of happiness and confusion.

"Yep, you're going home."

Erica gave me an oh-well-too-bad look, and I couldn't believe it. After all this time, my luck still sucked. I was pissed for the rest of the night. I was sexually frustrated in the worst way. My hormones were going cannonball and the only remedy was the feeling of release brought on by a girl between my legs.

The Control Room officer dimmed the lights to signal lockdown and I began to see the whole incident as a sign. What if Erica just so happened to have that pack? It was possible. Judging from her appearance, I'd say no, but sometimes you never knew until you felt the burn. I decided that maybe fate had looked out for a change. I felt so strongly about the ominous close-call that I again set my mind on celibacy- until I was out.

I fingered myself before I went to sleep, massaging and pulling my clit while I thought of all my old favorites and how they used to lick and suck me to orgasmic bliss.

———

The day finally arrived for me to go to court. It was me and five other girls in all. As always, I was last, and when I got in the courtroom I looked at the judge and the D.A before taking a seat beside my attorney. A young black woman named Ms. Grier. I heard through the grapevine that she used to be a probation officer in Clayton County. Judge Carver was an old fat white man with grey hair, slightly balding, and probably in his mid-fifties. Word around Metro was that he was fair, so I wasn't trippin'. Two things that I silently hoped to myself, though, was that no one had pissed him off before me and that the fair label he'd acquired was obtained through facts and wasn't just another inmate lie.

The D.A. pushing for a conviction was also a black woman, Laura Farrar. She looked to be somewhere in her mid-thirties. She was brown skin, short, and wore her hair in a bun. She wore an all-black Michael Kors dress with matching heels. Kind of cute. Her attitude just seemed fucked up. Like the type who was from the hood but her uppity parents somehow made a way for her to receive better schooling, so she felt she was above the inferior low and middle class. She probably only dated white men. It wouldn't surprise me. She obviously didn't care too much for her own race. You would think she would empathize with me on at least a minimal level.

I shook my head as I watched her prepare the paperwork that might very well be the notes that solidify my name on the roster down the road. I shook the thought. No need to think negatively. Juvenile made me nervous because there was no jury. It was all basically up to the judge once the facts are heard. I sat there before Judge Carver in my RY attire with my hair in a ponytail. When I looked around at the visitors in the courtroom, I saw Redd all kicked back looking hard. He smiled at me and threw his head back, the national head movement that every hood in America used to say "What's up?" I smiled back then faced the front.

As my case was brought before the judge, the D.A. began bringing up my past delinquent history as a problem child. She stressed the fact that even though I was a young lady, she saw me as a threat to my community. She then went on to say that it was the court's duty to the same community as well as her own to protect their well-being by ridding me from society and placing me in a Youth Development Campus to modify my behavior until the day of my twenty-first birthday. She brought up my not so benevolent conduct while being housed in Metro, topping it all off with the truckload of complaints made by the group home. When she brought up how I had killed Darrel, Ms. Grier objected and went in for the kill.

"She was protecting her family, Your Honor! The state doesn't have enough evidence to convict her. Which is why she got dropped to Juvenile. We can't hold her any longer. Not legally."

"She's right," Judge Carver said, shocking me to the core.

The D.A. was desperate. "Your Honor, I- just give me a little more time."

"You had two years. That's long enough as it is, even considering the circumstances. We have no choice but to release her."

I couldn't believe my ears. I swore they were playing tricks on me. I thought for sure I'd be walking away with some type of time today. Come to find out, their key witness, Daisha Hunter, couldn't testify. She was missing.

"Miss. Love," Judge Carver said. "You slid by this time young lady but you won't be coming here next time. You'll be an adult facing consequences far more severe so I suggest you get your act together. Since you have no guardian, I will release you on your eighteenth birthday into the Independent Living Program."

He slammed his gavel and the court was adjourned. I was so happy I could've kissed him, tongue and all. I felt like a Jew after hearing the announcement that World War 2 was officially over. For the last two years, Metro had been the setting of my holocaust. It was over now. I was so tired of being around these ratchet ass hoes, it made no sense.

When I got back to Metro RYDC, I told everybody I was going home, they were even shocked at the outcome of my case. Ms. Johnson and Ms. C were elated at the news of my once-in-life good fortune. I could tell Ms. Johnson's joy was authentic despite me calling her my enemy only months ago. She never treated me differently. Ms. C looked out on the food tip, sneaking me free-world grub whenever she felt she could do so without getting caught. Ms. Johnson and Ms. C were both God fearing women who kept me in their prayers and rescued me from lockdown more times than I thought they should have. We'd grown close in my stay here. My memories of them will never fade, I knew that. I loved them both like the grand-mothers I never had a chance to meet.

I went to my room, laid back, and thought about what I was gonna do when I got home. The money I'd make, the 'fits I'd roc, the cars, the women, all type of shit. I knew it was time to switch the game up. Either that or go harder. I was at a pivotal point in my life. With a clean record, I could get my GED, go to college and from there the sky was the limit. If something happened to go wrong and I ended up back in the trenches scrapping corners out a pot, I'd always have the streets to fall back on. What did I have to lose? The street was a door that never closed.

Unfortunately for me, the people I surrounded myself with and the things I devoted my life to were perfected through the dedication of my time. It had subconsciously become the only door I knew how to open. I could never acknowledge within myself the fact all other options intimidated me. My heart was waist-deep in the game and I had developed a strong inhibition toward all other avenues.

I summed up my incarceration as an outcome of part time thuggin'. With the right approach I could achieve success through this life I'd come to love. Without a shadow of a doubt at the right angle, I felt I could obtain the finer things without ending up dead or in jail. This time my actions would be thought through to the smallest detail. This time I'd go all in or not at all.

CHAPTER SIX

DIFFERENT APPROACH

(2010)

On the day of my release, I was placed in the Independent Living Program. I had to stay in a house with three girls and four boys. Not all of them were supposed to be living here but they didn't seem to give a fuck. It was alright with me as long as they didn't get in my way. I needed my space, all of it.

The get-up was a five bedroom, three-bathroom house. It was located off Pleasant Hill, right around the corner from Hillandale where I grew up. Memories were everywhere and with them was the life I left behind. I was happy to be back. Redd took me to get my nails, toes, eyebrows, and hair did. If he would've made me choose, I would've singled out my hair. It was almost to the middle of my back and it needed deep conditioning. I was looking rough. By the time Redd and I left the Spa, however, I looked rather ravishing. From there we headed to a tattoo parlor on Tara Boulevard. Bruce and Chino. They were brothers who made an honest living. The shop belonged to Bruce, the older brother. Chino had just done a three-year bid. I requested Bruce but he was in the middle of an appointment, so I hopped in Chino's chair. After he and Redd talked numbers I got tatted on my arm, from my wrist to my elbow. It was a portrait of Pam Grier, the original Foxxy Brown. Yea, I got it like that.

That night Redd, Polo, and I hit the club. VIP status fasho. Redd talked to someone and got me a wristband so I could attack the bar at my own discretion. The Ritz 2 was an eighteen and older joint. The next day he took me on my official Welcome-Home shopping spree. Polo tagged along as we went from *Macy's* to *Neiman Marcus*. When we arrived at Lenox Mall, we had already cashed out at *Nordstrom* and *Saks*. The trunk and backseat of his burgundy SS Impala was designer bagged to death. I looked at all the different logos and shook my head. Poor Polo. He looked so uncomfortable back there. With everything on Redd, I couldn't seem to tell myself no. That and the fact that my only socially acceptable outfit had been worn at The Ritz 2 the night before, and was still being worn now. Coming from someone who wouldn't be caught dead in the same outfit twice in one week, he understood.

I need clothes like trees need sunlight. At the moment, my pockets were like deflated inner tubes on a ten-speed mountain bike. It didn't stop niggas from trying their damnest to stunt. I wasn't checking for them though. I was looking to snatch up one of their high maintenance girlfriends. I was looking for a hat store that strictly sold hats when I walked by the music store and heard T-Pain's *Can't Believe It*. "That's my shit," I said, leaving Redd and Polo in my dust in my attempt to catch the bus down memory lane. I half jogged, half ran to the back of the store where the speakers blared my '08 anthem- and there she stood, five-six, golden bronze skin, a short do, and a body that screamed gym membership, swaying her hips to the song that brought back so many memories for me.

Her eyes were closed and she was moving her hand seductively across her body like a video vixen. It made me wonder where she was from. The colors she rocked were so odd to the eye... turquoise, lavender, orange, and lime green AirMax's graced her small feet. Her orange skinny jeans cupped her ass and gave way to her all black Nike shirt, with orange letters across the front. I could tell her hair was done but in what style remained a mystery. She wore a turquoise bandana over her head. If not for the subtle gleam caused by the cuts in her necklace, I would have never noticed the small, gold V chain hanging just below her collarbone.

When she opened her eyes and realized I'd been watching her, a smile ignited across her face. I smiled back. Mainly because she had me zoned out on her enticing sway and sensual curves, but also because I knew I had her.

"Not shy, I see." Not that she had a reason to be.

Her smile widened. "Not at all."

I knew off the rip that she was originally from up north by her accent. She said *all* like *oohl.* I looked her over. "Is that right?"

Her expression said, *Damn right, and you know it.* My eyes caught the album barcode scanner then shifted to the CD she held in hand.

"I guess I know who's responsible for playing my '08 love anthem. You might as well have been calling me by my government the way that song got my attention."

She laughed. "Word? Well, yo my bad, ma. I wasn't tryna hypnotize you but this my joint right here. They played it as a Flashback video yesterday on *106 & Park*, and I just had to come get it. I used to float around on an air mattress in my fava's swimming pool with the song on repeat. Now just the song alone is enough to bring about the feeling of peace and relaxation."

I nodded. "That's what's up. It's like that with me, too. It takes me back to a time where life seemed a lot less complicated, you know what I mean?"

"Mos Def."

We were surrounded by shelves loaded with CDs and cassettes and from the looks of it, there weren't many artists you couldn't find. Shoppers came and went as they found their own personal album.

"So, you're from Harlem?" I asked.

She shook her head. "Manhattan. My fava's from Harlem."

"How come I've never seen you here before? You new around here?" I asked, trying to get a read on her.

"Hell nah, yo. I moved down here a year ago after I graduated from school. I needed a change of scenery. Somewhere I'd be a stranger and free to live my life without the unwanted input of people who think they know you but don't," she paused. "I should be asking you that question though. I'm here all the time. I practically live here. That makes you the new face."

"Guilty as charged." I said. We laughed. "So now that it's established I'm the guest, would you mind showing me around for the day?"

She extended her hand. "My name is Violet.

"Kush." I shook her hand.

We talked and strolled around the mall getting to know each other. We bumped into Redd and Polo in the food court.

Without her noticing, Redd passed me a few hundreds so I wouldn't be walking around flat-face broke. Just on the strength of principle. I found out that Violet was a stripper at a club in Atlanta called Platinum 21. She had left the Big Apple for the Peach state in pursuit of happiness after her mother was killed, in a home invasion and armed robbery. Her father had become too suffocating afterwards, dictating her every move out of fear until she became fed up and took the next flight out. She was nineteen and most of all she was all for the money, like me. She was bad, too. I couldn't stop imagining what her face would look like in ecstasy. I had to have her. I could tell from her demeanor that she might end up a permanent at my camp. Fine, down to earth, and about her bread. She was an answered prayer, who could prove to be an asset. If my memory served me correct, Hispanic women were some of the most loyal females I'd ever come across. I got her number before leaving the mall. I'd get to know her some other time. I was too busy basking in Redd's let her in my world right now.

Redd spared no expense on my Welcome-Home shopping. I guess he appreciated my loyalty. After I got my wardrobe right, it was once again back to the basics. Business. Redd said he had the right nigga in pocket to make shit pop. A nigga named Bear, he had some major moves lined up. All we had to do was put a crew together. So far it was just Redd, Polo, and myself. We needed another female and I had just the right girl in mind. A bad bitch just itching to get her hands on some paper. For now, I had to focus on getting my pockets right.

The lick that would put me on my feet was Big Rod. He'd given me hope, following my daddy's death, then he'd taken it away, showing me the ways of a lying, disloyal ass nigga. The idea came to me the other day when Redd and I ran into him in the parking lot at Old National Discount Mall after snatching up a few mixtapes from the bootleggers. It was a cloudy day, he was leaning up against a Chevelle smoking a Black and Mild. At first, he just looked familiar. I barely recognized him and probably wouldn't have if it hadn't been for someone calling his name from across the parking lot.

I approached him. "Hey, stranger."

"Richelle? When you got out?"

"Last week," I told him. "So you know I need some fuckin' with. Set me straight on a lil somethin' till I get right." I already knew what he was gonna say before he even responded. I just figured I'd give him a chance to redeem himself.

"I got you next time, baby girl. Shit ugly right now, though."

I nodded, shot Redd a look and kept pushin'. I tapped Redd and gestured toward a jewelry store that was in the plaza. From the jewelry store, we watched him enter Old National Discount Mall.

We shot straight to the car and waited for him to come out. Twenty minutes later he did just that. We followed him around College Park for hours. I was ready to just hit him for what he had and take it to Fuwah, but he made a stop at a house that made me pause. I remembered the house. It was a tan house that sat on a corner in Thornton Woods. Daddy used to take me there all the time. I clearly remember he had brought me there in a rush not too long before he'd been killed. He put some work in the floor in the closet upstairs under a plank marked with a crescent moon shape chip. It was a stash house, one that Big Rod was apparently still using. I was surprised, but he was always a creature of habit. Still, I had to be sure.

I borrowed a pearl white Chevy Malibu from Fuwah and began watching the house. A green and grey Nissan Altima rode by often. After several days, I peeped it as a security detail. The Nissan passes every hour. The house across the street kept watch from a window upstairs. His moves were random. Something was definitely going on. There would be no security if there was nothing to protect. With that, I decided to strike.

Big Rod's face card was A-1 around College Park. He had a reputation for bussin niggas who played with his check, but I didn't care.

———

Redd was nowhere to be found when I decided to strike, so I picked up Polo. I figured if Polo was now a member of the crew, I might as well get used to him. More importantly, I needed to get a feel for his methods and ways of thinking. Thornton Woods was a fairly quiet neighborhood at night so we had to be extra low-key. I cut the headlights and brought the Chevy to a slow creep before pulling along the curb in front of a bando. I'd done my homework thoroughly, memorizing the security setup. I had it down to the T.

The bando was six houses down from the stash house. We peeped the scene for any deviation in the security routine. With the driver and the guy in the house on Big Rod's payroll, any slip-ups and it was over with. The Nissan made its hourly rounds while every so often the look out across the street peeped out the blinds.

"So," Polo asked. "When you tryna take flight?"

We both had our seats let back. "When the Nissan pulls off, we need to be in and out within ten minutes with whatever he got up in there."

Polo nodded. "I say we pull around to the street behind the

spot and cut through the back yard. Ain't no telling when that janky ass lookout might hit the blinds. It'll be just our luck, nah mean?"

I was impressed by his observation. The lookout's post checks were random.

"Good idea."

Polo pulled out a box of Newports, took one out and, fired it up. I cracked the window and he exhaled a cloud of smoke then said, "You don't like me too much, do you?"

"I don't know you not to like you."

"You don't like new faces, then."

"I don't trust new faces."

Polo hit the cigarette and blew the smoke out the crack in the window.

"So you don't trust me?"

"You're not a new face. I just don't know what you're about. Besides, I owe you one."

"Well, technically, you owe me two, but who's countin'?"

I was caught off guard. "Two? What's that supposed to mean?"

He smiled, flicking the butt out the window.

"I taught your friend Daisha a magic trick. She was having a hard time disappearing, so I helped her get it down pat. And from what I hear, she's mastered it."

"So I've heard," I said, playing it cool.

Talk about underestimating. Here I was slick jealous of Polo and Redd's *kick it*, and the whole time I owed him for putting in the work that saved my ass. Once again, Redd had proved to be on point in his judgement.

"Right on time," Polo said.

I sat up just in time to see the Nissan ride by. Polo pulled his seat up. "Let's do it, Kush."

I crunk the car up and eased away from the curb, whipping around to the street behind the stash house. Polo grabbed the duffle bag off the back seat and we hopped out, jumped the fence and, ran between houses, making a beeline to the stash house's back window. Polo pulled a glass cutter from the duffle bag and used it to cut a large circle in the kitchen window above the sink. He sucked the circle out of place, sat it aside then stuck his hand in to unlocked the window. We wasted no time climbing inside.

"Where the light switch in this motherfucka?" Polo asked.

"What the fuck, Polo? We can't turn on no lights. That's a dead giveaway. What happened to the flashlights I told you to bring?"

"Flashlights? You ain't said nothing 'bout no flashlights, bra."

I took Polo in for a moment. With his light skin and athletic build, he had that look that you'd see and automatically categorize him as a young man with his mind set on a future in some type of sport. His dreads were now to his shoulders covering the *Zone 3 Dill Ave* tattoo laid across his neck.

I sighed. "Fuck it. Just follow me."

I headed upstairs with Polo in tow. I was trying to make as little noise as possible and to move swiftly at the same time. Polo pulled out his phone in an attempt to illuminate our steps with his screen light. It wasn't much, but it helped. In the safe room, I went directly to the closet, tossing aside shoes and boxes in search of the plywood with the crescent moon chip. I was sweating bullets. I could feel Polo waiting to exhale.

"What we looking like on the clock?"

"We on Campbellton Road with thirty seconds left till we hit Da Burg."

"What?"

"Maaan, we thirty seconds from having three minutes left, Kush. Come on, you ain't been gone that long."

I was in no mood for games. "Bring the light closer," I said.

Polo closed in and I had to literally force myself to slow down and meticulously examine the planks.

"Come on, Kush. I see the tracks. Tighten up, shawdy." There was doubt in his tone.

No one wanted to be the orchestrator of a blank trip. I decided in a split second to rely solely on my other sense. The phone light was just too dim. There was no way I could see. Frantically, I began to run my fingertips up and down the wooden planks in a frenzy.

"Forty-five seconds from Bankhead."

"I know, okay? I got this. It's here, I just- let me do this!" I snapped.

Frustration had my nerves on edge. If I didn't pull this off, this move would do more than make me the inside joke of many smoke sessions to come. It would leave me financially unstable. I wasn't as paid as most people believed. I needed this. Asking for handouts wasn't my stilo. I'd been home almost two months now, plotting endlessly. I loved Redd like a brother, but I was sick of being his passenger. At the end of the day, I'm still a lady. I needed my space.

Seconds from a real live bitch fit, I felt something like sanded wood against my raw fingertips. I ran my hand back across the plank- and there it was.

"I got it!"

"Yeah." Polo was rather impatient. "You said that a minute ago."

"No, nigga, I got It. Watch out, watch out! Let me get right here. This closet ain't but so big. The plank lifts your way."

"Aight, come on, let's get it. We done wasted enough time. We gotta slide like thirty seconds ago."

"Thirty seconds? Polo- what the fuck!"

I was tearing at the wood, trying to work my nails into the crack.

"Aye, Kush. That ain't no issue! I told you I got you, aiight? We ain't come here to leave empty handed. Let's wrap this up so we can catch out. Fuck these niggas, we ball. Trust me, they ain't talkin' 'bout nothin'."

I tuned Polo out to focus on the task at hand. I was blowed, but there was a time and place for discrepancies. A few more tries and at long last the wood was up and before my eyes laid my next shopping budget. I went from edgy to euphoric.

"Look at them motherfuckin wheels!" Polo shrieked excitedly. He sounded like MC-Eiht.

There was weed in vacuum sealed plastic, two Ziploc bags full of X-pills, three bricks of cocaine, and old rubber banded money. With no time to lose, we began throwing everything in the bag. In our rush, I almost missed the envelope that fell from one of the Ziplocs. I picked it up and examined it.

"What is it?" Polo asked.

"I don't know."

"Well, pocket that shit. We gotta dip!" Polo said, throwing the duffle bag over his shoulder.

He didn't have to tell me twice. I pocketed the envelope and we tore it down. Back at the Chevy, I resumed driver status and we were on our way.

Amped wasn't the word, the rush from the turn in fortune was like a high. We came to a certain calm at the light on 138 and 85. We decided to add up the spoils at Polo's auntie's spot in Pointe South Apartments. I wasn't really familiar with the area so that was right up my alley. I didn't need nobody tryna be all up in my business.

Polo broke the silence. "Aye, my bad about that earlier, too. I was wrong. I ain't too real to admit that."

"I ain't stressin'. Just don't let it happen again."

The light turned green and I made a right onto Highway 85. Polo was quiet so I looked to my right to find him staring at me.

"What?"

He smiled. "You really think you have nuts sometimes, don't you?"

I shrugged. "Who needs nuts when you got guns."

We were adding up the lick work when I remembered the envelope in my pocket. After excusing myself, I headed for the bathroom to see what it was. On the front of the envelope were the initials *JR*. There was a letter inside. In my mind, I just knew I held the letter that would expose Rod's plug.

Aye folk,

Surprised yet? Yea that's right, I know what's going on. From the beginning, I gave you my loyalty no matter what it dealt with. Why? Cause you my brother. At least I thought you were. You've been using us from the start. What I thought was love, I now see for what it is. So yea, I got a lil something for the road, but only what I deserve. From now on, I'll do my own thing. Damn that money. Brothers don't do brothers like that.

From my heart to my trigga,
Rich

I stared at the signature. I couldn't believe it. This letter was written by my daddy, but when? *How?*

Knock! Knock!

I fumbled, dropping the envelope to the floor.

"What's up?"

"I'm finna take the Chev up to the Shell up the street to grab some Swishers real quick. Green light?" It was Polo.

"Just hurry up. It's getting late and I got shit to do tomorrow."

"Aiight, say less."

When the shadow from his feet departed from the door, I picked up the envelope. The initials of whoever had crossed my daddy stared me dead in the face.

CHAPTER SEVEN

GETTING MY HANDS DIRTY

T he next day things went on as if I'd never found the letter penned by my daddy. Finding the person it was addressed to was on the top of my to-do list. The letter had to be at least nine years old. The envelope was somewhat dingy. Just how long had it been ducked off? *Ecstasy hadn't been out that long, had it?* I wasn't exactly sure but I intended to find out. Big Rod had some explaining to do. It may not have been him, but whoever it was, my daddy had looked at them like a brother.

Within a week Polo had sold the work from our lick. Neither one of us had the clientele to break it down, so it was sold wholesale to some big timers his uncle did business with. With my pockets looking better I had Violet take me to a Lexus dealership in Morrow off Mt. Zion Boulevard. The day before, Polo bought a dark green Cadillac Escalade. I wanted to get my shine on too. I copped a red Lexus with cocaine white interior.

It was time to induct the last member of our crew. I had the perfect individual in mind. I gave her a call and I could tell she was surprised to hear from me. I told her to meet at the Hibachi Grill on 138. When I stepped out of my car and saw her, I was impressed. She was really doing it up for the summer. Her hair was straight with a bang, reminding me of the hot new rapper Nicki Minaj. She wore open-toe sandals, red skinny jeans, with an Aeropostale shirt.

She smiled and hugged me. "Oh, my, God! How have you been?"

"Fine Keisha. I'm home at least."

The plaza parking lot was full and a steady stream of traffic rode by on S.R 138. We walked in Hibachi's and stood in line. There was one customer ahead of us.

"Yea," Keisha said. "I just wrote you a letter the other day, cussin' yo' ass out for not writtin' me back. When you got out?"

"Uhh, about two months ago, now."

She sucked her teeth. "And you ain't been called me?"

"I had to get on my feet first. I couldn't just pull up on you with you all sexy while I'm looking Like Judge Carver's big toe."

Keisha laughed. "Well, you look good."

"You look good yourself."

We placed our orders, took our seats, and talked over Kung Pao chicken, egg rolls, and shrimp fried rice. I was sure she would be down, but I didn't want her to know the move if she wasn't, so I tested the waters. Confident that she was game, I gave her the rundown.

"So, where did you come up with all of that?" She asked once I finished.

"I didn't. We did as a team. Don't worry, though. You'll get a chance to add your two cents."

"Who is Bear?"

"He ain't the Feds, I'll tell you that."

Keisha dropped her head, absentmindedly stirring her rice. "You know him?"

I winced. "Not exactly. He told Redd he knew of me, though. I think he used to do business with Fuwah before I got jammed. I meet him tomorrow."

"I mean, are you sure he's good people, then?"

"Redd trusts him. That's enough for me."

"Well that's definitely not enough for me, but I trust your judgement. So what you need me to do?"

"Well for starters, we need to learn how to strip."

"Girl, I'm from The Grove. I been knew how to do that."

"No, professionally," I said. "I got a friend who works at Platinum 21."

"That's fine."

After we ate, we spent the rest of the day catching up and discussing the plan in depth.

Polo and I went to an upscale hotel just off the highway near the airport in East Point to pick up some money from someone who owed him. We took Polo's Escalade and arrived there at three in the afternoon. We came prepared, armed, but we collected without incident and was almost back to the whip when I heard someone call my name.

"Richelle?" they said. "Richelle, is that you?"

I started to take off. The only people who called me by my government these days *was* the government. What cemented my feet to the ground was the familiarity in the voice. My eyes needed to confirm. I lost trust in them for a moment. In no way could I believe my eyes. My heart stopped.

"Mama?"

"Hey, baby."

She tried to hug me like she hadn't seen me since Sunday morning service instead of since I was in 5th grade.

I took a step back and she paused. I looked her up and down like she was crazy. She looked a hot mess. Even worse now than I remembered. Being grown and have come into my shape, I realized how much I resembled her the way she looked before my daddy died. We could've been twins. Now with her matted down hair, dirty clothes, and sunken face, she was more the emulation of a Fulton Industrial crack whore.

"What you want?" I said.

She cracked a nervous smile. "You ain't happy to see your mama?"

I didn't respond. I just stood there looking at her. Polo, who had initially stopped to make sure there was no trouble, continued on his way to the truck.

She filled the silence. "My baby looks so grown now. I been hearing a lot about you."

"Oh, yeah?!" I snapped. "Well, what exactly have you heard?"

Caught off guard, she dropped her head and began twiddling her fingers.

"That you 'bout your money and you don't take no shit."

"Whatever," I said.

With no other words for a woman who'd become no more than a stranger to me, I headed for the Escalade.

"Richelle, I -mama sorry baby. I swear I was coming. I just-I...," she followed me to the truck.

I hopped in and closed the door. I rolled up the window and told Polo to step on it. I had enough of that family reunion for the day.

That night I laid in my bed and cried. I thought mama may have been killed trying to get her next high. I even dreamed one night that someone in Darrell's family had killed her as retribution for my actions. The whole time she's been running the streets like she never had a daughter. Was I not good enough? Just the thought alone hurt so bad. A part of me wished she was dead. At least then she would have a reason for not coming back for me.

––––––––

Redd and I finally went to meet Bear. My head was still throbbing from all the crying the night before, but I managed to pull it together. Bear's establishment was a big white house off Camp Creek. No mansion, but definitely not your average pad either. Redd knocked on the door, and I adjusted my shirt to conceal my strap. A fair skin cutie opened the door but was pushed aside by a short, swole black ass nigga with a bald head. He wore a tank top, cargo shorts, and some black, white and grey 95's. His Spurs snapback matched his shoes. Tattoos covered his entire frame. "Da fuck authorized you to answer doors 'round dis mu'fucka?" he growled. "You betta go find yo' ass somethin' safe to do."

The girl hurried off in her outfit that left little to the imagination. Bear smiled, flashing his golds. "What the play is Redd?"

"What's poppin?" Redd responded.

Bear looked at me. "What's up, Kush?"

"Hey," I said.

"You look different," Bear said.

"Um, have we met?" I asked.

Bear smirked. "Knew your father." He stepped aside. "Y'all come in."

We followed him and my breath was taken away by the interior design. There were marble floors and crystal chandeliers all around the house. At the end of the foyer, there were French doors that led to the living room. We took a seat on the Italian furniture. From what Redd told me, Bear sold drugs, had a few hoes on the strip, and had done eight years of fed time. He was cutthroat and would kill anyone who came between him and the almighty dollar.

"Y'all want something to drink?" Bear asked.

"No disrespect," I said. "Let's just get down to business."

He smiled. "You're direct. I like that... I like that a lot."

He grabbed the glass of wine from the coffee table beside the couch he was sitting on, took a sip, and cleared his throat.

"What you're about to get in may cost you your lives. You fucking with the big dogs now, not some little street punks. So you better come correct," he looked from me to Redd then placed the glass on the table and continued. "Let's get this money."

Bear went on to tell us about the first lick. The target's name was Chess. He had been copping major work from Bear and had just recently switched connects. He had a Haitian plug and was becoming a thorn in his side. Bear made it seem like Chess was biting the hand that fed him, but it was all a money thing in my eyes. I didn't care either way. As long as I got paid it wasn't my place to analyze his motives. Bear filled us in on what Chess was capable of and gave us an estimate of what we'd strike for. In the process, cuts were discussed, and a non-negotiable agreement was established. The actual details of the heist were left to be tactfully worked out by the crew. He gave us two weeks to prepare. This was a whole new ball game and we had to be ready. It was like Redd said: In this game when you slip, you fall hard.

CHAPTER EIGHT

PUSSY, MONEY, WEED

Polo cut his dreads off. He and Redd made the news and were wanted for questioning about a home invasion. Surveillance footage was mentioned, but so far no one had come forward to identify them. Redd too much ain't care. He didn't even cut his dreads. He said something about not going out like Sampson, whoever that was.

Kiesha and I had been hanging around each other a lot lately. She's become my first platonic female friend. I took her to get her first tattoo. She was scared at first but ended up getting *Love's A Bitch* on her left wrist. Keisha even helped me pick out my apartment, a one-bedroom in Camlot. Three month in the Independent Living Program had been more than enough for me.

Violet began teaching us how to dance like professionals. It was fun, and every time we practiced it was lively. While Violet demonstrated, Keisha and I would make it rain on her. Sometimes I would get wet and start getting freaky right in front of Keisha. I guess Keisha really wasn't bi. She was always saying things like, "Y'all need to get a room, y'all some big ass freaks!" One night after Keisha left, Violet and I were chillin' in my bedroom when she started telling me about a friend of hers she wanted me to meet.

"She's not bi, though," Violet said. "She's strictly-dickly."

I smiled. "If I want her to be she will."

Violet returned my smile with one of her own. There was never any pressure with her. She knew I talked to other girls. She didn't care. Besides, she knew I was right. When I met Violet, she was only curious but she'd never been intimate with another woman. I taught her how to eat pussy. Now that's all she wanted to do. At that moment, she looked as if she wanted to do just that.

"I got a surprise for you," she said.

"What you waiting on, then? Show me!"

"Okay, wait right here."

She left the room and I rolled me a fat one and fired up. The idea of what she had in mind got me wet. She returned in nothing more than stilettos and a translucent lavender two-piece. She made her way, seductively, over to me. Panties drenched, I sat on the edge of the bed and took another hit of the blunt. She turned and started bouncing that ass in my face.

"Slap it!" she demanded.

I did.

She moaned. "Harder."

I complied.

She laid me back and whispered in my ear with her strong New Yitty accent. "I'm finna eat you so good."

I took the last few hits of the blunt as she began undressing me. My feet in the air and legs spread apart, she grinded her pussy to mine. It felt so good. I was powerless to stop the moan that escaped my lips.

"Mm-hmm," Violet cooed. "You like that don't you, babe?"

"Yes," I said.

All I could do was lay right there and grind with her. When she went down on me, I thought I would lose my being.

"Aahh mm-hmm, right there. Eat that pussy," I moaned.

She just kept licking. Licking me so fast I grabbed her head and wanted her tongue to go deeper as I grinded my pussy all in her face.

"Damn, Violet!" I screamed. "Oh God, I love it." She was eating me just right.

"I'm cuming, I'm cuming! Oh, God, I'm cumming!" I panted.

I gripped her hair as tight as I could and looked down at her eating me. I couldn't believe she had my toes curling. She held me until I stopped shaking. We kissed passionately as I savored the taste of my juices on her lips. It tasted good.

"My turn."

I got up and made my way to my closet to grab something I was given by another female. Violet saw the strap-on and began stroking her clit. I put it on, went over, and she grabbed it and started sucking. I pulled her hair back from her face so I could see her eyes. She sucked and moaned simultaneously. She spit on it and sucked it all off. That shit had me so turned on, I bent her over, face down, ass up, and went to town.

"Aah, damn Kush!" she yelled. "Fuck me mami, fuck me!"

I slapped her ass. "Say my name."

"Kush," she wined.

"Who fucking the hell out you?"

"You Kush. Ahh, baby, You! Kush, I want you baby. Damn, I want you."

I slapped her ass again.

"I'm finna cum, "I'm finna cu- " she cried.

I kept pounding that pussy.

She came and we laid up in the bed talking. She kept telling me how sexy her friend was and that she wanted me to meet her. I told her right now she was the only one on my mind. I kept seeing her pretty little face between my legs. A few kisses and a couple of suggestive stares later, we popped off round two.

———

The next morning, I was talking to Violet in the parking lot right outside my apartment as she got ready to leave, the sun was already shining bright. Out of nowhere, Big Rod pulled up in a tricked-out black Denali with gold trim and skirts. Standing right outside Violet's driver side door, I was suddenly conscious of how defenseless I was. This was supposed to be a simple farewell so I had left my strap inside. I was transfixed as his window came down.

"Yo Kush," he called. "Got a minute?"

He had my full attention. "What's up?"

Violet watched our exchange.

"Shiiid, take a ride with me real quick. I got something I need to show you."

Knowing what I'd done, I debated whether I should ride or not. There was no way he could know my involvement and I didn't want to show signs of character deviation, but paranoia was a mufucka. At the same time, this could be a test... or a setup. I decided to take a chance, but not before leaving some bread crumbs. I leaned in Violet's window and told her to call Redd and tell him I was going for a ride with Big Rod.

I hopped in his passenger seat and other than initial small talk at first, there was little to almost no conversation. We rode to the sounds of T.I's *Paper Trail* album. We pulled into the Thornton Woods subdivision. My pulse quickened. I shot a nervous glance in Big Rod's direction. I wasn't strapped or ready for any bullshit, so I'm glad he didn't catch it. He parked in front of the stash house Polo and myself had struck only weeks before.

"Who lives here?" I said.

"You."

"We just left my house. What the fuck you talkin' 'bout?"

He popped the locks and opened the door. "Come on, I'll show you."

I followed him to the front door, looking around for anything that seemed out of place. I saw nothing. Big Rod opened the door and we entered the living room. Straight ahead was the kitchen and to my right were the same stairs Polo and I had used the night we hit the spot. I didn't notice that night, but the house was actually furnished, a little too furnished for a stash house. Then again, it would make for a good cover-up.

"See anything that belongs to you?" Big Rod asked.

My heart was beating like a mufucka. Did I slip and leave something that could be traced back to me? I was about to run, then I saw something familiar. Me as a baby- in the form of a framed photo on the wall. I approached and looked closely at the other pictures. I knew some faces, while others were only vaguely familiar. I was lost. "How did you get these? Who are these people?"

"They're your family," he said.

"Then how come I've never seen them before?"

"You have," Big Rod said. "Probably just don't remember."

A picture of an elderly woman resembling the famous African-American poet Maya Angelou caught my eye. Her smiled was graceful, her features strong and proud. I grabbed the picture off the coffee table.

"Who is this?"

Big Rod smiled. "The reason my belly so big."

"Who?"

"Ms. Dorthy, your grandmother. She loved you. You were the daughter she never had. Life's just fucked up and she died from cancer a year after you were born. This was her house. She left it to your father when she passed. Now it's being passed to you."

"But from who?" I said, placing the picture back on the coffee table. "My caseworker told me neither one of my parents had written wills."

He walked into the kitchen, and I followed him.

"They didn't," he said.

"Then who's giving me a house?"

He grabbed some papers off the counter. "That, I honestly don't know. I'm just doing what I've been paid to do the last eight and a half years."

"And what's that?" I asked.

"What I've been told to do in any matter concerning this house."

Big Rod handed me the papers. Among them were the deeds to the house with my name on it. Utility information, as well as the previous owners of the property.

"Who is Rontavious Devon Love, Jr.?" I asked.

The name was listed as the previous owner.

"Your uncle, Junior. Your Daddy's brother. Remember?"

I stared off into space thinking hard, but as much as I wanted to remember, I couldn't put a face with this so-called uncle of mine. What did catch my ear, striking a bad vibe, were the words, *Junior and brother.*

Brothers don't do brothers like that, my Daddy had written.

As that final sentence crossed my mind, so did the initials on the front of the envelope I found with the stash: *JR.*

"Whatever happened to him?" I asked.

Big Rod shrugged. "No one knows. He disappeared right after your father's murder. With him being the only surviving adult relative, the house was transferred to his name. He must've took it upon himself to handle it or the house would've been repossessed by the city. You were too young to make mortgage payments then."

It still didn't add up. "So, my daddy gets killed, my uncle claims the house and some anonymous person takes over the mortgage while my uncle disappears?"

Big Rod nodded. "Sounds crazy but, shiiid, hell yea."

"Then this same anonymous person gives me the house after paying you to watch it for nearly a decade?"

"Right," he said. "Now you wanna see your daddy's old room?"

I sighed. "Sure, lead the way."

We headed upstairs and down a hallway, passing two rooms and a bathroom. I was overwhelmed with a sense of irony. My daddy's room was the same room the stash was ducked off in. Inside his room were two dressers and a bed. I looked to the closet but the door was closed.

"I was supposed to give you the deed on your eighteenth

birthday, but with that Armed Robbery you managed to get yourself caught up in, I didn't know how that was going to play out. Then I ran into you a little while ago, but before I could get everything together, someone broke in and tore up the floor." He opened the closet.

I looked inside and saw the hole that was left. The wooden floor planks were stacked neatly in a pile beside some shoes. I looked around the rest of the room, taking in everything as Big Rod continued talking.

"A lot of people over the years have tried to break in. Some were successful but they never get anything, simply because there's nothing to steal. Nothing of value that I know of. I guess they figured I use this house, well, check up on it. But I don't stay here, so they must've thought this is where I keep my stash. They couldn't have been farther from the truth. My dealings with this house are strictly business and out of loyalty. I grew up with Rich, we started kickin' it hard in the ninth grade at Banneker High. Yo daddy was a leader, Kush. A real standup guy and the glue that held the team together. When he died, so did most of the other's ambition."

There was a photo on my daddy's dresser. It was a picture of him, Big Rod, two other guys, and two females. A club photo. They seemed to be celebrating something. I could tell because Daddy and Big Rod were both holding up two bottles apiece and everyone else was flashing money. One of the girls in the photo was caught off guard by the camera, gazing up at Daddy intimately. It was subtle but it was there. There was another framed picture beside it. I picked it up. It was Daddy as a teenager with some dark skin skinny guy.

"That's Junior right there," Big Rod said, noting my observation.

I didn't respond or asked questions. I simply stared at my uncle. The whole time I had been thinking the letter I found was addressed to someone my daddy looked at like a brother. I was wrong. It really was his *actual* brother. It was my uncle Ron.

CHAPTER NINE

SHOWTIME

Two weeks flew by and it was time to set everything in motion. Keisha and I were at The Ritz 2 in VIP, courtesy of Bear. We were at our little private table with two bottles of Grey Goose. We had thoroughly gone over what tonight's encounter was to establish and we were chilling, waiting for Chess to show face. The question wasn't if he was coming, but when. Redd and Polo were tailing him. From our table, we had a clear shot of everyone coming and going. I was turned up to the max and so was Keisha. She wore her hair in micros, sporting a tight black mini dress and a pair of black stilettos to match. I had on a spaghetti strap baby-doll dress with some *fuck me* pumps, and my hair was in curls around my shoulders. Left and right, niggas were offering to buy us drinks, but we were here on business and the two don't mix. So, we declined.

My phone vibrated. It was Redd letting me know that our marks were en route. I showed Keisha the text and no more than ten minutes later, we saw Chess and his whole crew. Six of them. I never seen Chess before tonight, however, I was able to pick him out immediately. He was tall, dark and, handsome. He rocked a bald head, sported a full, close-shaved beard and looked as though he worked out. He wore a casual white V-neck with blue jean Tru's that complemented his butter Timbs. The platinum chain and ice clusters in his ear and his pinky gleamed for attention.

"Showtime," Keisha said.

We made our way to the dance floor and got our dance on. We watched them in their section. It was getting late and by midnight the club was thick. Back at our table, I noticed Chess eyeing me. I watched him through the shifting crowd. We locked eyes, and he averted his gaze. I held mines steady, waiting for him to look my way again. He did, and this time I smiled and averted my gaze. I leaned over to Keisha who was sipping Grey Goose from a glass.

"Is he still watching me?" I yelled above the blaring music.

She shot him a glance. "Yep, sure is."

I tossed back a few shots, got up and headed to the bathroom with a walk so sexy, niggas and bitches were breaking their necks to get a look at my ass. Everybody was watching but I was interested in one set of eyes. I passed Chess's section and hadn't made it far before someone took my hand from behind. I turned to find none other than Chess himself. *Bingo!*

"Whazzam baby?" he said.

"Hey."

He released my hand and stood at a comfortable distance. "I don't mean no harm or nothing, but I just had to know your name."

"Who wants to know?" I asked.

He chuckled. "Excuse me but uhh, Chess. My name is Chess."

"Kush," I said, reaching my hand out. "Platinum Kush."

Chess accepted my hand. "Nice to meet you. And if you don't mind me asking, how'd you end up with a moniker like?"

"I could ask you the same thing. Chess is definitely not the name your mother gave you."

"It's not," he smiled. "My name is Chester."

"Kemoni," I said, giving him my middle name.

He paused, noticing his crew hawking me. "Let me buy you a drink."

"Sure," I said.

We made our way through the crowded club. At the bar, we ordered drinks and got to know each other. Everything I told him was false. I had no way of knowing if he was lying or not, but it wasn't important. Just as he began to tell me about life growing up in New Orleans, Keisha tapped me on my shoulders.

"Baby," she said. "I'm ready to leave."

"Oh, you gay?" Chess asked.

"Bisexual," I said.

I turned back to Keisha. "Hold on baby, I'm talking to someone."

Keisha sucked her teeth and rolled her neck. "Since you caking with some nigga, I'm finna go find me one, too."

She turned to leave but Chess stopped her. "Well hold on, wait. I got a partna that can keep you company."

"Naw, that's fine. I'm okay." Keisha said.

Chess wasn't taking no for an answer. "Come on lil mama, let me show y'all a good time. Everything's on me. Anything y'all want just name it and it's yours."

I looked at Keisha. "What you think?"

She shrugged. "I guess so."

"Come on then, I got just the right partna in mind for you." Chess smiled. "Oh uhh, Kemoni, you with me."

Chess was used to getting what he wanted. He thought because he had money he couldn't be touched. I couldn't wait to show him otherwise. Who better for the job than a dime-piece who knew niggas like she knew her own pussy. We went over to their section and kicked it with his crew. They smoked and drank good. Keisha and I didn't drink much. We had to be on point.

Back in his section, Chess wasted no time finding Keisha someone to chill with for the night. Some Brandon T. Jackson lookin' ass nigga named Damien, who just so happened to be Chess's, right-hand man. I winked at her as I enjoyed getting in Chess' head. It tickled me how he thought he was running game when in all actuality I held the reins. I was running circles around him and was about to run off with his sack. He didn't deserve any money anyway. His head was so far up his ass he really believed he could have any woman he desired. When I got through with him, he wouldn't trust so recklessly again... if he lived to trust again.

"When can I see you again?" Chess asked when it was time for us to go.

"I don't know," I said. "I'll see you around."

"Don't be like that," he said.

"Be like what?" I said. "What you want me to say?"

"Look, Damien and I are planning on having lunch at Frank Ski's downtown tomorrow at noon. Join us. My treat. What d'ya say?"

I agreed, we exchanged numbers, and the next day we met downtown. My goal was to get Chess wrapped around my finger without sex. I was sure he had dealt with his fair share of gold diggers, so I had to come correct with my role. People want what they can't have. I didn't act innocent, but my dislike for dick made my front more authentic. At the same time, my presence led him to believe he would get something he wouldn't.

Chess dealt with a lot of out-of-state business, so I couldn't play him as close as I wanted. But whenever he was in town, we went out on the regular- plays at Fox Theater, upscale restaurants, the Georgia Aquarium. He was into art and we often went to museums and antique auctions, so I had to act interested in all that bullshit.

He opened up about himself, mentioning his military background and his intelligence operation in Iran. A spy blew their cover, they were taken hostage and tortured for Intel, but he didn't fold. Later rescued, he was awarded for his bravery, then he retired and used his military savings to invest in dope.

It wasn't long before he started offering me money. I never took it, but on the rare occasion when I did accept his gifts, I was modest about it. I had to keep up my image. It paid off, though. Chess lived in an upscale neighborhood off Bethsaida Road in Riverdale. It just looked like money over there. He started inviting me to spend the night, insisting that I sleep with him even though we weren't fucking. He said it didn't matter, he only wanted to hold me at night to show me we were bigger than sex. I saw through it, but I went along. He had hope. I couldn't afford to have him in his feeling about some pussy. So even though I got tired of waking up with a hard dick pressed against my ass, I continued to sleep with him.

I woke one night and he wasn't there. I found him in his study, fiddling with a safe in the wall. His expression, when he saw me, went from shock to apprehension to panic. He rushed out then we went back to bed. He was hiding something and I knew it. From then on, on the nights I slept over, I would play sleep and he would often sneak off. On the nights I followed him, it was always to the study. No longer was the door opened, though. He kept it locked, even when he wasn't there, which made me even more suspicious. It crossed my mind to have the crew storm the house, guns blazing, but there was no point. We could torture him all day and he still wouldn't talk. His medal of honor and the scars on his body were a clear reminder.

I was ready to put a plan together, but I needed more help. Damien had to be seduced to our side. Keisha was complaining about how clingy he was but we could use that to our advantage. I talked to her and she went to work getting in his head. Pride and ego could be a man's downfall. I was counting on it. He was closest to Chess. If anyone knew the combination to that safe, it was Damien. We needed him to flip.

Keisha's sudden change of heart had him wide open. I began working my magic from the other side as well. Whenever Chess was out of town, I would go out with Keisha and Damien, flirting with him the whole time to test the waters. I was subtle so I'd have room to finesse if he ran his mouth. He didn't. He flirted back, and I took the next step by insinuating that the three of us together was something I could get used to. I began to hint that Chess was all that stood in the way. The seed was planted. All that was left was execution.

I *bumped* into him and Keisha at the Frozen Palace. He brought her there to have a good time, but Keisha and I had money on our minds. We clung to him all night, going out of our way to make him feel like he was *The Man*. Then at the bar, with Keisha's okay, I made my move.

"Listen, Damien," I said. "I want the three of us to be but Keisha and I need a boss."

Damien's face twisted into a sneer. I could tell he was offended. "Oh, I got money!"

"Not as much as Chess," I retorted. "You can't even afford your own plug. He treats you like a shrimp when you should be the one big dawgin' it! We can help you. You'll be the H.N.I.C. With Keisha and myself by your side, what more could you ask for?"

If he said the wrong thing he was dead. Keisha had a pistol in her handbag. He just didn't know.

Damien looked at me hard. "How we gone do that?"

"What do you think our best chance is?" I asked.

"I asked you first," he said.

"So?" I countered. "I asked you last."

Damien narrowed his eyes, smiled, then took a shot of Remy to the head. He placed the glass back on the counter.

"I think we both know what needs to be done. The problem is neither of us wants to say it. A lack of trust, maybe. I don't know, but I need answers if we gone pull this off. So what's up? What has to be done?"

I shot Keisha a glance before I answered.

"There can only be one king on each side of a Chessboard. That said, someone has to go."

He nodded. "Chess."

I had to be sure he wasn't trying to bait us, so I let him do the talking. He ran a plan by us and from the sound of it this wasn't the first time he'd thought of crossing Chess. He said that whenever Chess wasn't home he had several street soldiers standing guard. We would have to hit him while he was there. He even went as far as to say Chess had to be killed, although I had been thinking the same thing. Redd and Polo had peeped the street soldiers' presence, there was a way around it all but I was still suspicious of Damien's intentions. When he told me the exact location of the safe, I knew then that he was really with the move. He mentioned us needing some outside help, so I took over from there. I could tell he liked it. By the end of the night, I had the combination. It was an act of treason that would've shocked Benedict Arnold himself.

———

After months of coaxing and finessing the night had come to put the plan in action. Keisha and I were in my car headed to Chess' house with Redd and Polo following close behind. Wearing trench coats, we got out making our way to Chess's front door. I knocked and moments later it was answered by a member of his crew. In the living room, there were five niggas including Chess and Damien.

"Hey baby," I said to Chess. "You ready for your present?"

"You sure you want to do this, bae?" Chess said.

It was ironic that he would ask such a question. It was as if he knew what was really about to go down.

"Anything for you," I said.

Chess smiled.

I looked at Keisha. "You ready, baby?"

"Yea."

Chess's crew stood around wondering what was to come. There was a table in the middle of the living room floor. Keisha and I dropped our coats. I had on a flaming red two-piece with black and red stilettos. My get-up revealed my tattoos. Keisha had on an all gold two-piece with glass stilettos looking just as good. I undid my hair, letting it fall down my back. They went crazy. Damien hit the music and *Nasty Song* by Lil Rue started playing. We stood on top of the table and put what Violet had taught us to use, dancing and shaking our ass like the shit was brand new. We were winding and gyrating our hips to the music as niggas stood in amazement, drooling and gripping their crotches. Everyone was into it. We gave them quite a show. I was almost lost for a minute.

Forty minutes later it was time for the grand finale. I looked at Keisha and put my hand behind her neck, bringing her in for a kiss. Our tongues danced. I tugged at her bottom lip with my teeth as we caressed each other sensually. We stopped, looked in each other's eyes for a second, and then started back again. I thought I was trippin' when I heard her moan. Keisha was straight to my knowledge. I opened my eyes and saw Damien looking out the window and flicking the blinds. That was Redd and Polo's queue. I got back to playing my role.

BOOM!

The door flew open. Keisha and I broke our kiss and got down to business.

"What the hell?!" Chess yelled.

I turned around just long enough to see him catch a slug to the dome. Gunshots rang out while Keisha and I ran upstairs to clean out the safe. I put in the combination, opened it up, and saw nothing but money and dope. I let out a sigh of relief. I was half expecting Damien to be full of shit. By the time we finished, the gunfire had ceased. There were four dead bodies to greet us when we came downstairs. Redd and Polo were tearing shit up while Damien stood in place by the window.

"We good," I said. "Let's ride."

Keisha ran to the kitchen to cut the gas stove on.

Redd nodded. "Aiight, let's dip."

Polo tapped me, then jutted his thumb at Damien. "What about him?"

"Yea," Damien asked. "You got my cut?"

I grabbed the pistol off Redd's waist and pointed it at Damien.

"What you doin'?" he asked incredulously. "We had a deal!"

"We did, didn't we Damien?" I asked rhetorically. "Too bad there's no honor amongst thieves."

I let six shots go and Damien's body hit the floor limp. We set the house on fire and dipped out the back door. Completing our first mission as a crew, we rode off into the night as flames began to rise and lick the stars.

CHAPTER TEN

OLD MEMORIES

W e had it all. To say we were on top would be an understatement. The crew had struck ten bricks and one hundred-twenty racks. We gave half the bricks to Bear as agreed and sold him the other half for the low. As for the cash, we split everything down the middle. We were ballin' out. I was so happy. I gave my mama a band and told her to fix herself up. I could've given her more but for all, I knew she was still on drugs. As much as I wanted to hate her, she was all I had left. Eventually, I moved her into the house my daddy left me.

I was finally getting a taste of how rappers and ghetto fabulous hoochie mamas felt when they came up. For so long I had looked out my window seeing everything I dreamed and wished for. Now it had manifested right before me. I had it but didn't know what to do with it.

The other day I laid my money out, spread it across the bed and fucked Violet on top of it for the hell of it. The mall was our second home and whatever Violet said looked good on me, I bought it. The crew and I went everywhere together. We were about our bread and Bear kept us on the move. For the next three years, we jugged hard.

———

2013

Violet was now a dancer at *Magic City*. Which was where I'd be partying for my twenty-first birthday. Too bad Keisha couldn't come. Her brother got shot at a dice game so she was down at Grady. Tonight it was just me, Redd, and Polo. I was anxious to have some cuties shake their ass in my face. I had five bands ready to throw. Some new rapper named Chief Keef had everybody rockin' mismatch designers. I was feeling the movement with my tan *Vera Wang* blouse that matched my *Louis Vuitton* shoes. I had a Louie bookbag on my back, a Louie rag tied around my neck, and a four-carat diamond bracelet on my wrist. I was turned up!

When we stepped in the club I wasn't shocked, but I was amazed at how many bad bitches in sexy lingerie and stilettos were walking around. A sexy Latino mamacita walked by and blew me a kiss. I made a mental note to start coming here more often. I fuck with bad bitches. I know what they look like and they were damn sure in here. Magic City, where fantasies come true. We took our seats at a table reserved for us at center stage. I was eager for Violet to perform.

"Happy Birthday, Kush," Redd said.

"'Thanks."

"Yea, we gone do it big tonight!" Polo said. "Aye, say, lil

mama," he grabbed a dancer gently by the wrist. "It's my sister's birthday. Go treat her right, and we gone bless you."

The dancer was thick in all the right places. She had double-d titties, an ass that put most Georgia peaches to shame, and shoulder length hair. A pretty smile and smooth chocolate skin. She approached me, turned around and I started placing bills in her black latex booty shorts. She had *Bunni* written across the back in diamond-studded rhinestones.

A waitress came over to our table looking like Lisa Ray in Player's Club. "Can I get y'all anything?"

"Yea," Redd said. "A bottle of Grey Goose on ice for each of us."

Redd had always been a man of few words. When he did speak it was in a calm and collected tone. His demeanor was similar to Big Meech's in that Raw Report DVD.

"Is that all?" she asked.

"Naw," Polo said. "While you at it, gone and pour yo' self a drink and put it on the tab."

"I'm fine. I don't drink on the job sweetie, but thanks anyway." She said walking off.

Polo looked at Redd. "I found who I'm leaving with tonight."

The music changed and Bunni left as the dancers hit the stage, shaking ass all in our faces. *Bandz A Make Her Dance* by Juicy J was playing as the girls worked the poles. I was throwing money but I was really waiting on Violet to show face so I could make them hoes green with envy.

The bottles came and I started guzzling everything in sight. There was a girl with a booty so fat, so fucking big, I wanted to grab and play with it. I slapped it and it was soft too. She had a star tattooed on her right cheek. I was hypnotized by the way she was making it jump. She had roses on her lower back and butterflies fluttering up and over her right shoulder that added to her sex appeal. Redd and Polo were causing a severe thunderstorm in her world. She was paying me no mind.

Violet came out. My baby was looking so sexy. I started throwing good dollars at her. She smiled when she saw me. During my thunderstorm, someone yelled, *Star*. I looked back, they were talking to the girl with the star dancing on Redd and Polo. She turned around and I felt like I'd been hit by a freight truck. I had to be trippin'. My heart skipped a beat and my feelings came rushing back from the dead. It was Chelsea. I got up and rushed to the bathroom.

Everything seemed to move in slow motion. I was in a state of disbelief. I ran to the sink to splash water on my face. I had to clear my head. I couldn't stop thinking, *why now had she popped back up in my life?* After all the time that had passed, *why now?* It had been five years and I hadn't even heard anything. It was as if she had disappeared off the face of the earth. But here she was at *Magic City*. It must be some type of magic up in here for real. It took a minute, but I got myself together and went back to the table.

"You aiight?" Redd asked.

"Yea," I lied. "Had to piss real bad. Must be the liquor."

"I want that hoe with the star on her ass to come back," Polo said.

As if on cue, she walked back over to our table and I knew I wasn't tripping. It was Chelsea. I didn't know if I should go hug her or box her in her shit and drag her all through the club. Violet walked up.

"Hey, baby," she said. "This is my friend I was telling you about for years."

What the fuck? This world is entirely too small.

Chelsea stuck out her hand. "Hi, my name is Star. Nice to m-Kush!"

"Yea, what's up?"

Redd, Polo, and Violet looked shocked.

"Y'all know each other?" They asked simultaneously.

Chelsea and I looked at each other, and what took place next caught me completely off guard. She gave me a big hug.

"I haven't seen you in so long!" she exclaimed. "You look so pretty, oh my God!"

I still didn't know what to say, so I didn't say anything at all. I was wondering how much time I would do if I beat her ass to sleep in here.

"How y'all know each other?" Violet asked.

"We grew up in the same group home when we were younger," Chelsea said.

She forgot to mention that we were first loves. Hell, she even conveniently left out the fact she set me up to get jumped. Some things are better left unsaid, I guess.

"So, what you been up to?" Chelsea asked me.

I wanted to be rude and just fall off in her shit, but I kept my cool.

"Shit. Just ballin' on these lames and shittin' on these hatas."

She laughed. "I see you haven't changed much."

"Not at all."

Chelsea kicked it at our table for an hour or so, then Polo, Redd, and I split.

"How you know her?" Polo asked once we were in the car.

"Old friends," I said, leaving it at that.

Redd knew what was going on. I could tell by his facial expression he knew exactly who she was. We all went to school together.

111

I decided to stay the night at the house my daddy left for me rather than my apartment in Camelot. It was my way of spending time with my daddy on my birthday. I'd been doing it for the last three years since receiving the deed. Whenever I was there, I slept in my daddy's room. Mama had the master bedroom down the hall.

Over the last few years I had dished out thousands of dollars to private investigators in an attempt to track down my uncle, but it was as if he had vanished. I felt like Big Rod knew more than he let, but I was convinced of his loyalty. The money and work I had stolen was my daddy's. Big Rod knew nothing about it. Daddy had obviously written the letter and ducked it off with the work, then had gotten killed before he could move it. I had a good mind to believe my uncle was behind my daddy's murder. Big Rod didn't think so. I believed that if he wasn't the killer, then he knew who was. I laid in bed. I couldn't sleep. I thought about Chelsea and the lick Bear had set up for us in Jamaica. I was ready to go.

CHAPTER ELEVEN

DOPE SOLD, MONEY FOLD

"Somebody ain't coming out of this bitch alive!" Bear said.

I'd never seen him this mad. The crew had just gotten back from Jamaica and we'd stopped by his crib to give him his cut, sell him some dope, and discuss the next move. He was chumping off sixteen of his workers as they stood lined up in the three-car garage when we walked in.

"Let's just leave and come back," Keisha said.

Polo sucked his teeth. "Fuck that, he ain't talkin' to us."

Redd spoke. "Exactly."

Polo sat down the briefcase and leaned up against the wall, while Redd and Keisha stood by his side.

"Which one of you bitch ass niggas stole my money?" Bear yelled. "Nobody got nothing to say? Aiight then, everybody in this bitch gone die!"

We stood watching him eye the sixteen menacingly. All of a sudden he busts out laughing. "Kush, come here!"

Reluctantly, I walked over to him, wondering what he wanted with me.

"Which one of these niggas you think stole my money?" he asked.

I couldn't believe he asked me that. I didn't even know these workers. "Just pick one," he said.

I looked at Redd's expressionless face then I looked at the faces of the accused. Daddy always told me you can see and smell fear in a nigga. Only the guilty would be afraid. I pointed.

"Them two."

"What the fuck? Hell naw!" they protested in unison.

Bear chuckled. "Good choice."

I could be wrong. If so they'd die for simply being some scary ass niggas. If the actual thief did get away, 1 commend him. He wore a mean ass poker face in circumstances of life or death. Bear reached for his pistol as they begged for mercy. These niggas were some real live bitches. If I knew I was going to die, I would make sure to go with my respect.

"Both y'all come here," Bear told them.

Once they were standing before him, he blew the first one's brains out. Brain matter was all over the floor. He wasn't bull-shitting.

"Please, please, please don't kill me!" the last one standing shrieked in fear.

Bear laughed. "Shut up, fool. I'm not finna kill you."

The last one standing looked shocked.

"I knew he was the one who took my money the whole time. Ain't that right?" Bear said, pointing at the worker and his brain matter on the floor.

"Y-ye-yea, he took it," the last one standing said.

He had to be the dumbest nigga since MC Hammer.

"Lay your hand out on the table," Bear said.

"What?"

"Nigga, you heard me!" Spittle flew from Bear's mouth.

The last one standing looked sick but he did as he was told. Bear reached for something and when he pulled it out I was shocked. It was a machete. The last one standing began begging and pleading once again.

"Shut the fuck up!" Bear yelled. I ain't gonna kill you. Ima just teach you a lesson about having sticky fingers," he grabbed the nigga and swung the machete.

CHING!

The last one standing released a sickening cry and fell to the floor crying and gripping his hand. Blood gushed from his wounds, staining his shirt. His good hand clutched his deformed one to his chest. He writhed in agony as a pool of blood began to form underneath him.

I don't know if what I was seeing was something I was ready to witness, even if he did deserve it. Bear had chopped four of the man's fingers off. I stared blankly at them on the floor and didn't know how I felt about pointing them out and subjecting the workers to such cruel and unusual punishment. I mean I wasn't a saint myself, but goddamn! Fingers don't grow back.

"For anyone who think they gone double-cross me or pull some cutthroat shit. I feel sorry for you." Bear pointed the machete at the rest of the workers. "Somebody clean this shit up!"

Bear walked by and motioned for us to follow him inside to what he considered his own personal oval office. It wasn't oval at all but it was fairly large. It reminded me of the room Tony Montana's sister was killed in minus the balcony.

In front of Bear's desk were two chairs. He took a seat

behind the desk, and Keisha and I took the others. A black leather couch was along the wall but Redd and Polo chose to stand. I wasn't feeling a long ass discussion.

"So, what you got for me?" Bear acted as if chopping fingers was something he did on the regular.

Polo sat the briefcase on top of the desk, opened it and turned it to face Bear.

"That's three Ki's. The cut we agreed on," Redd said. "You know we too tough don't deal with coke. We really just fuck with the gas. The crew, that is."

Bear smiled. "Sounds about right. However, I'm extremely pressed for time, so let me give y'all the next job. That is if you find yourself still interested by the end of the briefing."

We remained silent and he continued.

"The job will be your most lucrative yet dangerous move thus far. Lucrative as in you stand to gain millions. Not apiece but split five ways between me and the four of you. You follow me?"

We all nodded and he proceeded.

"The dangerous part is this next move involves the Haitian Zoepound. I know y'all are fearless but I also want you to take into consideration how much money is involved. It's sure to be heavily guarded and won't be taken lightly. Definitely not as easy as the Jamaicans. The trip may take longer than the week y'all spent there as well. So far y'all have proven able to hold up your end. It's been nothing but good business between us. I'd like to keep it that way. I don't like fuck-ups. I have other crews more than capable of pulling the job but I've been tuned into y'all campaign. I much rather put the money in y'all pockets. If you feel I'm in over my head and this is a little too much for you, let me know. Anything other than success won't be tolerated. So, barbeque or mildew?"

Polo was amped with no hesitation. "Shiiid, throw that bitch on the grill. You know I'm wit' it!"

Redd simply nodded while Keisha looked at me as if my decision would be hers. I thought about how high the stakes were this time and about how with each job the risks seemed to increase. I thought about the guy whose head was just blown off right in front of me and his peon partna, whose fingers had been chopped off in Bear's garage. I thought about Ross and Cunningham and the million or so other pigs that would love to see me under a jail. Last but not least, I thought about Judge Carver's last words of warning to me three years ago. I realized just how deep in the game I actually was. All I saw were dollar signs. Money was my motivation and there wasn't a single method in psychology that could change my mind. I was sold.

"I'm in."

———

I rode in silence with today's events on my mind. After we had agreed to the job, Bear gave us an even more in-depth rundown. He informed us that it would take a while to set everything up. I was curious how he got the inside info. I was on 285 when my phone rang. I didn't recognize the number. I turned the radio down. This better be good. I was missing Big Tigga's Trendy Topics on V-103.

"Who is this?"

"It's me, Chelsea."

I was stunned for a moment. "Whaddup?"

"We really need to talk," she said.

"About?"

"I can't say over the phone. Just... can you meet me somewhere, please?"

"If I do it's gonna be later on."

She let out a sigh. "Okay."

"Meet me at the Applebee's at eight."

By eight I was pulling up at Applebee's. I brought an extra pistol for security. I'm a strong believer in the fact you can't make the same mistake twice. The second time it's a choice. *So why was I here?* I walked in and spotted Chelsea sitting at a table in the far-right corner of the restaurant by the window. She stood when she saw me, and I took her in as I approached. She had grown up since our days at the group home. Of course, her skin tone was the same, her hair as well. It was still light brown. Yet her petite frame had grown to a much thicker physique. She stood five-seven now with c-cup tits and a juicy booty. The navy-blue Polo shirt and tan tennis skirt she was wearing hugged her curves. On her feet were tan, white and navy-blue skippers. She reached out to hug me and I noticed her nails were done also.

"Hey," she said.

I hesitated, then hugged her. "Hey."

I didn't want to seem as interested as she did. She acted as if she didn't want to let me go. She finally did and we took a seat. It was awkward. I could feel the tension in my neck. I couldn't stop thinking about the time she set me up. How did she get my number was something to consider as well. *Violet could've given it to her.*

"So," I said. "What you wanted to talk to me about?"

"A lot," she said. "Damn, Kush, you look so different."

"What's that supposed to mean?"

"I don't know," she smiled. "I mean, I guess I thought you were going be a stud with a bunch of war wounds or something."

My eyes narrowed. "I got a war wound right here on my eyebrow where I had to get stitches because some girl I knew set me up."

Her smile vanished. "Kush, I'm sorry. I was young and dumb then. I loved you so much. You were my first love. I didn't even like girls but I liked you for some reason. It's just that when I saw you with Meeka that day, I wasn't thinking rationally. I just wanted you to feel the hurt and betrayal that I was feeling. But I was wrong. I acted out of anger and I've lived with that regret ever since."

It sounded good but I couldn't let her get to me. She held my gaze and continued.

"You don't know what I've been through since that day. You think I want to be a stripper, Kush?"

I stared at her unflinchingly.

I was going through hell thinking about that day." Her voice cracked. "I finally started getting my life together, doing something for myself. I relocated to Florida and worked at a hair salon for four years, getting paid under the table. I'm going to go to school for cosmetology so I can own my own business. Stripping is getting old. I even met this guy in Miami who I'm engaged to. I had just started to forget about you when I saw you at Magic City that night. At that point, all my feelings for you invaded my head. I went home and cried the whole night. That's when I realized that after all these years I still care about you. I started to think about what Violet would tell me about y'all relationship over the years, wishing I was in her place. Yet, I never even knew she was talking about you until the other night."

The dam broke and Hurricane Katrina was in full effect as

Chelsea cried me a fucking river. I couldn't stand to see her cry and it got to me. I needed to leave.

"I'm so confused right now," she said between snivels. "I don't like girls but, but- "

"But you like me?" I finished.

"No, Kush. I... I think I love you."

Damn. We'd never stepped this far from shore. I didn't want to let her get in my head but it was deep out here. Still and yet.

"I need to leave," I said and was on my feet.

"At least take my number."

"I already got it," I said over my shoulder.

I sat in my room that night, staring at Chelsea's number, wondering if I should call. Redd knew what happened that day. What would he say if he knew I was talking to her again.

"Fuck it," I said and dialed her number.

She was in bed with her fiancé when she answered. He was in from Florida on a business run. Despite the fact, I told her to come over. I heard her shuffling around and I got wet with anticipation. She was on her way. The knock on my door came a little after midnight. It crossed my mind that this could be a setup. I grabbed my pistol and made my way to the door in a white T, a white bandanna around my head, and some booty shorts. I opened the door.

"Kush, what the fuck?" Chelsea was visibly shook.

I tried to play it off. "My bad. I thought you was somebody else."

She laughed. "You that paranoid?"

"Naw, just being careful. Can't get caught slippin'."

"Oh... right." She looked hurt. Like she knew I was talking about her.

"Come in."

She stepped through the foyer. "This your place?"

I closed the door and made sure it was locked. "Yea."

"It's nice but it's cluttered.

"Thanks for noticing."

She made herself at home on the living room sofa. She wore open-toe sandals, some jeans, and a South Beach T-shirt.

"You want something to drink?" I asked.

"Yes, please."

I grabbed the Tampico juice out the refrigerator and turned around to find her standing directly in front of me.

I jumped. "What you doing?"

"You always had pretty eyes," she said, staring down the road to my soul.

I blushed and averted my gaze. She ran her fingers through my hair.

"And good hair too."

She grabbed the back of my neck to bring me in for a kiss. Our lips touched and hers were just as soft as I remembered, the softest lips I've ever kissed. Our tongues met and she squeezed my ass. Chelsea pulled back and caressed my face with the back of her fingers.

"Kush, I'm in love with you."

She grabbed my hand and led me to my room. I laid back on the bed while she stripped to reveal the sexiest body I'd seen in years. I took hold of her narrow waist as she straddled me with her thick thighs. I could feel my panties growing moist as she rocked her hips. She planted kisses on my collar bone then sucked on my neck. The combination caused a soft moan to escape my lips. She removed my shirt to find my nipples standing at attention. She sucked them and circled her tongue around my areola. I looked down to watch her as she slid my shorts off.

"Your pussy looks so good," she said. "Don't worry, I still remember how you like it."

She spread my legs and started eating my pussy. She was flicking her tongue rapidly. She slowed down and nibbled my clit. That made me go crazy.

"Aah, damn you eating this pussy so good," I wined.

She stopped licking and started slurping loudly, devouring my snatch. I held onto her hair as tight as I could and started grinding my pussy in her face. I stared at the ceiling and let her eat her way to my soul.

"You like it?"

"Yes, baby. Oh, yes!"

She inserted two fingers in my hot cave and finger-banged me as she attacked my clit. She came up for air and wiggled her index finger inside me. As if she was telling my uterus to come to her.

"Say what's on your mind."

"Damn Chelsea, I love you, I love you!" I shouted.

She was making me cum like never before. My toes curled and my eyes rolled to the back of my head. I held her hair tight, screaming her name at the top of my lungs. My legs couldn't stop shaking.

We laid in my bed as she held me tight, telling me that she loved me and she would never stop. I listened and thought about how my feelings for her had grown. I could feel it. That was the best head I'd had in my life. She said she had to go, but I didn't care. I needed to get my head right.

When she left, I found myself listening to some R&B feeling like a Class A Sucker. *Damn, what the fuck was wrong with me?*

CHAPTER TWELVE

DYING FOR REVENGE

Another month went by and we hit a lick in Gastonia, North Carolina on a storage complex. It was an inside job from Bear to put some money in our pockets, though we didn't exactly need it. A local drug dealer had some money stashed and we were given the scoop. In an all-white van, we made it past the access gate and pulled around. Using bolt cutters to disable the master lock, we were able to get into the storage bin. We were nearly through loading the van in what was supposed to be a free-band lick when two black trucks whipped in and four guys hopped out and opened fire on us.

One of the shooters had crept me from the side. I saw him at the last minute. He fired off a round and missed. Keisha got the drop on him and took him out. Had she not, it may have cost me my life. Redd spazzed, calling me stupid. Saying that I was letting Chelsea get in my head.

I had been with Chelsea every other day or whenever her fiancé was on the move. She knew me and Violet messed around, but what could she say? She was the one getting married. Violet told me for the first time that she loved me and would quit stripping just to be with me. I was beginning to believe a committed relationship wasn't a sensible move for someone who lived a lifestyle like mine. It's dangerous. Not just for them, but for me as well. I could fall victim to my crime all because my mind wasn't on the job. What irked me most was the fact that Redd was right. Chelsea had me fucked up-her and Violet.

Bear hit my line and wanted to discuss some things in person. We decided to meet up at TGI Fridays in Camp Creek Plaza. I got a call from mama as well. She said she was doing a little better. At least she was trying to kick her habit. She wanted to be admitted into rehab. I was happy but I didn't let it show. Seeing is believing. I told her to meet me at TGI Fridays as well, thinking to kill two birds with one stone.

I pulled up right after the sunset. It was 8:08 PM and I was prepared to get fussed at, even though my slip up had taken place nearly a month ago. I couldn't blame hime. I was still mad myself. The whole ordeal made me so mad I had been visiting a shooting range in the country since we returned. I refused to miss another shot.

I walked in and saw Bear at a table towards the back in the damn near empty restaurant. I approached and took a seat.

"Spit it out," I said.

Bear smiled. "You aiight? You look pissed."

"No, I'm not aiight. You finna do what Redd did and cuss me out, ain't you? Well, what's up? Let me have it!"

His eyebrows creased. "That's the past. This is now. It's time to put the Haitian move into effect. I already notified the rest of the crew."

"Oh..." I felt stupid. "My bad."

"No problem," he said. "Listen, Kush. This ain't no game. I need you focused. This is big money right here. Fuck all the other money that you been getting. You ain't never even dreamed of the kind of bread you finna eat. To pull this off, I need you."

I'd already spoke to Keisha so I knew what he was proposing. He was forfeiting his cut on this job. The move itself was more important. Bear wanted the Hattians out the way so he could connect directly with the plug and take over the Florida trap trade. This move alone would make him one of the biggest king-pins in the region. I wasn't complaining, though. He gets what he wants and we get our bread. Everyone wins.

"The most, how?" I asked.

"I'ma need you and Keisha to entice Zoe and his team," he said. "They tender under the zipper. Only thing is, it may take more than a month."

"More than a month?" I asked.

"More like six to ten."

"Naw, I'm straight."

"Come on Kush," Bear pleaded. "Think about it. If you back out then Keisha's gone, too. She values your opinion and you know it. Besides, I already said you can split the money four ways. You couldn't make half of this type of dough in a year working at a Fortune 500 company."

It was suddenly clear. All our previous missions were nothing to him. We were being tested in skill and loyalty, auditioning for the one mission before us now. Had we previously failed or gotten killed, it would have simply proven we were neither capable nor ready to take on the Haitians. The stakes were high. There could be no second attempt. Success had to come the first time around.

"Okay, I'm in."

"That's what I'm talking about," he rejoiced. "I knew you wouldn't let me down. Now check this out..."

As he put me on game, that feeling that I knew him from somewhere was nagging at me. It was odd, a familiar feeling. I knew I never met him so it couldn't be possible. We finished eating and talking business. Mama still hadn't shown face, she was full of shit.

When I got to my car, she was at the passenger door.

"Damn, I slid my phone back in my pocket. "I was just about to call you. Why you didn't come in the restaurant? You're not hungry?"

She shook her head. "No, not really. I'm just ready to get this over with."

I popped the doors, we hopped in and I pulled off, headed to the rehab center in Atlanta. An awkward silence filled the car. Mama had a distant look in her eyes. I started to ask what was bothering her, but I didn't know how personal it was and we definitely wasn't kicking it on that level. She stared out the window at the trees lining the highway. Traffic was slow and the streetlights highlighted her face in passing.

"So how long have you been hanging around your uncle?" she asked.

"My uncle's dead. What you talking about?"

She looked at me. "Richelle, I just saw y'all eating and talking when I walked in the restaurant. That's the reason I came to the car, so don't play dumb. I hate him and I just don't want to be around him. He took the only man I ever loved away from me and changed my life forever. He's the reason I am the way I am now- the reason you can't stand the sight of me. I mean I know I can't just- "

"Ma, that was a nigga named Bear. What you saying?"

"You don't remember who that is you just ate with?"

I was getting frustrated. "I just told you ma, Bear!"

Mama shook her head. "Richelle, that's your uncle Junior. The one responsible for the death of your father. Ron!"

A dam flooded with old memories from my past rushed me. My uncle.

That's why he seemed so familiar to me. There were pictures of him all through the house my daddy left for me but he looks so different. In the pictures, he was slimmer. He didn't have tattoos and he had hair. The other physical changes came from age. It was starting to make sense. It answered why he favored me out of the crew. Yet it didn't explain why he wanted daddy dead. His own brother. How had Redd come across him? Did he know? Was Redd in on it, too? No, I'm trippin'. We're the same age. Redd couldn't have been no more than eleven when my daddy died. None of this made sense.

"I don't understand." I said growing angry. "If you knew who killed daddy, how come you never said anything to the police? Why are you just now telling me?"

My mama started to cry. "Richelle, you don't understand. They would have killed me. I was all you had left!"

"That didn't stop you from abandoning me eventually!" I yelled.

"I know baby, but that was after I got strung out. I never meant for things to be this way. Your life or mine. I'm so sorry," she sobbed.

Anger fueled my momentum. "You got that right. The sorriest excuse for a mother the world has ever seen. A lousy spouse, too. You didn't love my daddy!"

SLAP!

SKUUUURT!

"How dare you!" Mama yelled.

I swerved on 285 from the force of the slap mama delivered to my face.

"Now I may not have always made the best decisions concerning us, but don't you ever doubt my love for your father! I wasn't one of those scheming bitches who hooked my wagon to his star for riches. I loved Richard."

I stared ahead at the road, furious as I hopped on the turnpike. "So, what happened?"

Mama tried her best to mollify her attitude.

"All I know is he made a deal with some Jamaicans. Things were good at first. Out of nowhere, everything fell apart. Your father wanted us to move to Virginia. He had some work and money put up but the same night we were to leave, he was murdered. A week later the streets started talking and everyone was looking for Junior but he disappeared. Tonight was the first time I've seen him in twelve years."

A few minutes later we were pulling up at the Rehabilitation Center. When I came to a stop I unlocked my doors.

"Get the fuck out my car."

There was a pregnant pause as she stared at me. "Richelle, I-"

"GET OUT! NOW!" I screamed.

Mama dropped her head and whispered, "love you..."

I stared ahead. I had nothing to say to her. In my eyes, she'd betrayed my daddy and left me for dead. She got out the car and I peeled off.

I weaved in and out of traffic crying. I could barely see the road. How could I have been so blind? I could almost feel daddy looking down on me frowning. I should have done my own investigation. I made my mind up about what I had to do next. I called Bear. "Yeah, this Kush," I said. "Meet me at Flat Shoals Park. It's an emergency." I hung up and shot towards Flat Shoals like a bat out of hell. Revenge was the rage fueling my motive. Nothing else in the world mattered.

From the shadows of the bleachers by the baseball field, I watched Bear pull up. I had busted the lights out the street lamps. I was ready to see him bleed. He stepped out of his black Rolls Royce with silver trim and looked around. He pulled out his phone to call me, and while his guard was down I revealed myself.

"Rontavious Devon Love, Jr.," I called.

He spun around quickly, his eyes grew to the size of UFOs when they met the barrel of my .45 Magnum.

"What did you just call me?"

"You heard me," I growled.

"What you doing?" his eyes shifted back and forth from my eyes to the barrel. "Put the gun down. You trippin'."

I looked him in the eyes with nothing but disgust.

"Before you die, I just want to know why you killed your own brother? You knew you were my uncle and never said anything."

"Richelle, it ain't like that. I love you like my own. I was gonna tell you, but now wasn't the time. So many times I wanted to tell you but why when I could keep you close and look out for you all the same. You wouldn't understand. I did so much to get to the top, you could've been killed all for retaliation."

He took a step toward me and I stiffened my grip on the trigger. He put his hands up to show he was surrendering.

"Richelle, I swear to God I didn't. Why would I kill my own brother?"

"You liar," I screamed. "You did it for power!"

"No. I didn't. I swear. Let me explai-"

BOOM! BOOM!

I put two in his chest. I shed tears as I walked up on him and looked down. Blood spewed out his mouth as he stared into the eyes of death.

He tried to speak. "It was-"

BOOM!

Headshot.

CHAPTER THIRTEEN

FUCKING WITH FIRE

The death of Bear became the enigma of the south side. Not a soul knew and no one was talking. I watched Redd's face to gauge his reaction to the news of Bear's unfortunate end but there was none. He simply stated that since we knew the details of the caper, we would proceed.

Redd had been acting strange since the job we had pulled in Jamaica. He would disappear for days, sometimes weeks at a time. Usually, I paid no mind to his moves but with the question marks surrounding his connection to Bear, my curiosity had been piqued. After a brief investigation, his disappearances turned out to be harmless. He was taking trips to and from Jamaica because he fell in love with the scenery of his origin.

Violet quit stripping and moved in with me. I was in that pussy every night. Just when things were beginning to get serious between us, Chelsea dropped a bomb on me.

"You told him what?" I said.

"I told him I didn't want to be with him anymore because I'm in love with you," Chelsea said.

We were sitting on the sofa in my living room, which looked better thanks to Violet. I got up and started pacing the room. *Why in the hell did she have to do that? Better yet, why did she always seem to have the most fucked up timing?* Months had passed since I knocked Bear off and the crew and I were headed to Florida to pull the Haitian job tomorrow.

"I can't help how I feel Kush," Chelsea said. "And I've learned to live with a few regrets, but I get the feeling that this would be one mistake that follows me for the rest of my life."

"But, why now?"

"I don't know!" she screamed then whispered, "I guess when your hearts on fire, some sparks may fly out of your mouth."

Seeing her in her present state revived a feeling in my heart I thought dead a long time ago. Compassion. I thought I loved Violet, but now I realized that I'd been trying to force myself to love her because I knew she genuinely loved me. I had love for her but I loved Chelsea more.

I sat back down on the sofa beside Chelsea and took both her hands in mine as I looked her in the eyes.

"If I come back, we're going to be together."

"You mean *when* you come back," she said.

I kissed her deep and passionately before pulling back. "Exactly."

———

The whole flight to Florida I thought about Chelsea and Violet. I kept picturing the look of betrayal that Violet would wear. At the same time, I imagined the same look of pure elation that my commitment would put on Chelsea's face. I thought about how Violet might feel towards Chelsea being that she had confided in her about her feelings for me for three years. I tried to reason that Violet technically had no right to feel any type of way due to me and Chelsea's past- a time before I never knew Violet existed.

Keisha and I managed to get seats beside each other and she made it possible for me to have a good time. Polo kicked shit, too. Redd, well... he was being Redd as usual. We got our grub on. First-class was a motherfucka. It seemed as though no matter how many times I made a trip via plane, the view from the sky never ceased to amaze me. The land looked sectioned off in squares. I was transfixed by the sun rays shining on white cotton-candy-like clouds. The peanuts were a luxury as well. I don't know why but they always taste better on an airplane.

We arrived at Miami International on Saturday afternoon after enduring the short one hour flight from Hartsfield-Jackson International Airport. The sun was beaming bright, it was hot as hell. We made our way through the shuttle and grabbed our luggage from the carousel. After renting two blue Audi A4 convertibles from Enterprise, we checked into the Ritz-Carton Hotel. Redd and Polo had their own rooms. Keisha and I shared a room as usual. The suite came with access to the hotel's indoor swimming pool, room service, a wet bar, and an ocean view.

After trying out the room service and showering, it was lights out. Tomorrow the games began.

———

The next day Keisha and I were on the beach and ready for work. From the outside looking in we were just regular vacation girls here to soak up the sun. South Beach was crowded for a Sunday. I guess real beaches kept this type of company consistently unless it rained. Atlanta Beach was alright but it was man-made and nothing like the real thing.

The scene was beautiful. Children were building sandcastles while their parents watched from under umbrella sun blockers. There was a game of volleyball going on while others were stretched out to sunbathe on towels. I took a deep breath. There was saltwater in the air, another thing absent at Atlanta Beach. A lifeguard was checking me out from his tall post. It was apparent that sunblock wasn't doing him any justice. He had a mean ass burn. His whole body was covered with red except for those rings around his eyes from his glasses and his trunks. Keisha and I walked along the beach looking good enough to eat. I had on a lime green two-piece. Keisha wore the same, except hers was black.

I took notice of seven Haitians walking together. Some had dreads, others had long goatees. None of them wore shirts, only watches, chains, and rings that gleamed, diamonds dancing in the sunlight. Everything else about them seemed Plain-Jane outside of that. They rocked cargo swim trunks and basketball shorts. I nudged Keisha and nodded in their direction. "That's them."

"You sure?" she asked.

"Positive. I've studied their pictures a million times. I'm on point."

"Alright," she said, pulling a frisbee out of our beach bag. "Let's do this. Go long."

The plan was to toss the frisbee back and forth before she tossed it in their direction, giving me a perfect reason to run into them. No more than five steps away from a job well done, a little kid toting a beach ball ran across my path and tripped me up. I fell face first in the sand. Embarrassed, I didn't want to get up.

"You okay?" someone asked in a thick Haitian accent as I got to my feet.

I was too busy brushing sand off my body to look up. "Yea, I'm fine."

He held out the frisbee. "I believe this belongs to you."

He was skinny but toned with low-cut coily hair, and skin dark as the nights sky.

I took it, noticing for the first time just how tall he was. I would have to stand on my tip-toes to kiss him for sure. "Thanks."

He smiled. "Don't mention it.

I turned around to walk off.

"What is ya name?"

I stopped and turned back. "Who wants to know?"

"Alonzo... but you can call me Zoe."

Lucky me. "Well, Zoe, thanks for your concern, but I'm seeing someone at the moment."

Zoe smiled. "I just want to know the name of the person who hit me upside the head with a frisbee."

"That would be my girlfriend." I pointed at Keisha. "And her name is Mona. Satisfied?"

"Not yet," he replied. "Name, please?"

"Julie."

Zoe nodded. "So, what brings you and your girlfriend to town?"

"Probably the same thing that brought you and your comrades," I gestured towards the rest of the Haitians. "The beach."

"You okay?" Keisha came up behind me.

"I'm fine, bae."

"Hello, Mona," Zoe said.

"Umm hey," Keisha said before looking at me. "How does he know my name?"

"I told him," I said. "I hope you don't mind."

"Not at all," Keisha said. "Does he have any friends?"

"Mona!"

"What?"

"Plenty." Zoe grinned and turned. "Dun-Dun!"

I shot him an incredulous stare. "Come on girl, let's go."

I turned to leave, and Keisha grabbed my hand. "Bae, wait. Let's see what they talking' bout."

A brown skin Haitian guy with waist length dreads and a thick beard approached us. The rest of his crew was posted with female friends of their own. A group of children ran past.

Dun-Dun gave Zoe a pound. He wasn't as tall as Zoe, but he had some height on him. "Whapun?"

"I have a lady friend who needs some company."

"Which lady you speak?" Dun-Dun asked, eying us both.

Zoe pointed at Keisha. "Mona in black."

Dun-Dun took Keisha's hand and kissed it. "Nice to meet you, Mona in Black."

Keisha smiled. "Please, just call me Mona." She gave a girly giggle.

Dun-Dun chuckled. "Of course."

Zoe and I began walking along the beach. His convo was on point but I had no intentions on anything real. Most of what I told him was lies. There was no way for me to tell if what he said was authentic or not so I labeled most of it as counterfeit. It made no difference to me anyway. This was just another job.

Zoe showed me up and down the beach. He asked was this my first time coming to South Beach. I told him yes and he explained to me that the beach was one long ass strip with clubs, restaurants, and shopping centers called Ocean Drive. He asked if I rode a jet ski. I hadn't, so he took me for a spin and we had a blast.

I genuinely enjoyed myself. By the time we reached the shore, his boys were ready to go. Keisha had been chilling with Dun-Dun the whole time but she didn't want to leave with them so she went back to the hotel. Hours later I found myself walking down the nearly empty beach with Zoe as the sunset. He asked if he could take me out to eat later tonight and I said yes. I asked if Keisha could come too and he was with it, saying that he was sure that Dun-Dun would like that.

I went back to the hotel and told Polo, Redd and Keisha what the move was. Keisha and I had overtime to put in so we got dressed and headed downstairs to wait for Zoe in the lobby. While we waited, Keisha and I filled each other in on what we knew so far, which wasn't much. We didn't want to seem thirsty for information and they weren't the type to offer. What we needed, we would have to get in to see.

A conservative looking young man wearing a tuxedo approached the front desk. "I'm looking for a Julie and Mona."

"We're Julie and Mona," we said, speaking up from where we were seated close by the bell-hop.

He looked at us as if he was checking to see if our description were right, and he was apparently satisfied.

"Come," he said. "Your ride awaits."

We walked outside and to an all-black stretch Hummer with silver trim, on at least 30-inch rims.

"Here you go," the driver said, opening the door and helping us in.

"We riding in this?" Keisha asked.

"Yes, madam, that is correct," he said.

Keisha and I were beyond excited. Neither one of us had ever ridden in a limo before. Which was kind of crazy considering all the money we had run through. I looked at Keisha, she looked at me and we smiled. Let the job begin.

I started seeing Zoe more and he eventually took me to his house and told me he wanted me to be his girlfriend, exclusively. I agreed though I didn't expect him to stop fucking with other bitches. *Kush* wasn't green by a long shot, but *Julie* would have to be, so I played along.

His mansion was big as fuck. It sat right on the coast of Miami with a dock for his boat. He used it to go back and forth to Haiti. I would go with him from time to time. It was beautiful.

Little Haiti was another story. The area where majority of the population was Haitian. The first time I went I witnessed a murder. A Zoepound member had been sent on a move with a hundred-round clip, when he returned it was apparent he hadn't emptied it. A young member in the ranks named B-Style killed him on the spot.

Zoe oversaw a club called Take One. It was The Zoepound headquarters and also where they kept a lot of stolen merchandise. They were robbing the boats on the ports and selling weed and coke throughout most of Florida, up and down the coast. On a trip, I met a Zoepound member named Red Eyes. He was a

Haitian rapper that Zoe was investing in. He was trying to clean up some of his dirty money.

Things started getting serious between us and fast. Zoe wanted some pussy and I was starting to see that there was no way around it if we were going to pull this off. I had to give it up. He was cut from a different cloth than Chess. I'd been refusing his advances and I could tell he wasn't going to keep going for it. So I made up my mind to let him have it on his next attempt. I hit the shower, when I came out he was on the bed naked and stroking his dick. I had nothing on but a towel.

"Come to me, Julie," he said.

I stared at his thick, black dick as I did what he ordered. I reached him and he grabbed me by the hand and put it on his manhood. With his hand over mine, he continued to stroke it as he closed his eyes and exhaled heavily.

"Lay with me," he said.

He pulled me down on top of him and started kissing on me. I wasn't into it at first, but I found my rhythm. He sucked on my neck and planted a kiss on my collarbone. He went down and I closed my eyes and spread my legs wide. I imagined that he was a girl, gripped his dreads, and rotated my hips as he ate me good. He came up and kissed me again. I felt him throbbing against my entrance and was struck by apprehension. When he started rubbing the head of his dick up and down my slit and against my clit, I placed my hand lightly against his chest

"Wait, Zoe," I said. He was so into it he didn't respond at first. "Zoe."

"Hmm?"

"It's been a while. Be gentle, okay?"

He kissed me. "No worries."

I closed my eyes as he lined his dick up with my entrance.

When he eased the head in, I was breathing through clenched teeth. He pulled out and slid back in. I couldn't help but think about Darrel. Before now, his dick had been the only dick to enter me. I felt myself drying up and I could tell Zoe felt it too because he paused in mid-stroke.

"What's wrong?" he asked."

I had to get it together. "Yes, I'm- I'm sorry. Come on."

He began slowly stroking me again and I did my damndest to go with the flow. I thought of all my sexual conquests and before I knew it I felt myself getting wet again. He increased his speed and I gripped his shoulders, my mouth forming an O as I took it. It hurt at first, then to my surprise it started feeling better, good actually. I couldn't believe I was moaning as he sexed me at a steady pace. I wrapped my legs around his waist and when he stroked me long and deep my breath caught in my throat.

He started pumping hard and fast. "You like?"

I replied by biting down on his shoulder, tasting the salt from the sheen of sweat covering his body. I held on tight as he pounded away. My tits were bouncing uncontrollably as he beat my walls. Then I felt it. I was about to cum. Zoe must have sensed it too cause he lifted my legs up and fucked me hard, encouraging me to cum for him. I threw my hips to meet his thrust and it hit me, wave after wave of ecstasy. Zoe pulled out, came on my stomach, and collapsed on top of me. I couldn't believe I just did that but it wasn't as bad as I thought it would be. I knew it wouldn't be the last time, either.

———

I was doing my thing and so was Keisha. We often met up on Washington Street at Club Madonna. In the girl's restroom, we shared what we knew. Come to find out, Dun-Dun had flown in a couple of days before we met them, when things went sour with his fiancée. He would still be in Georgia but Zoe had some business in motion and Dun-Dun needed to be closer to home. I told Keisha how Zoe and Dun-Dun were cousins and how Zoe and his mother was all he had left after the disaster in Haiti a couple years ago. She talked a little more agreed to meet up at a shooting range in Broward County this weekend.

I started moving work for Zoe. Every street nigga wants a bad bitch who's not afraid to get her hands dirty now and then. I was spoiled. To solidify my role even further, I was giving it up on the regular. I took that big, black Haitian dick like my life depended on it, which it kind of did. When he would stick his tongue in my ass and clean his plate, I squealed and squirted. Dun-Dun and Zoe got together often, and whenever they did, it gave me and Keisha a chance to work together. It was at one of these get-togethers that we decided it was best if Zoe and Dun-Dun were killed during the raid. For now, though we were proving our loyalty. We had more than enough opportunity, but we never pilfered a penny.

Zoe wanted me to stay with him, and I did just that. No one else lived with him but his mother. She had her own room on the west wing of the house. I got in good with her and watched Zoe's every move and to security as well. He had fifteen street soldiers.

I often called home to check on Chelsea and Violet. They were straight. They just missed me and couldn't wait for me to come home. Redd and Polo were having a good time, enjoying the Sunshine State. I would see them at times, watching me and Zoepound whenever we were out and about, I spoke to neither of them in public. We spoke over the phone every so often.

They were ready to move but I was trying to stress to them the seriousness of this lick and how important it is for us to strike suddenly and disappear without a trace. There was no way we could wipe out the entire Zoepound. I was still working out the details but I knew I would play a major part in their demise. There was no room for error. The slightest mistake and we'd pay with our lives. All of us.

I came home from the grocery store and walked in to find Zoe and five other Haitians out back hovering over some white guy. An accountant who had fucked them out of some money, he said. Right before my eyes Zoe cut one of the crackers' eyes out and placed it in an envelope with the intention of mailing it home to his mother. That along with a few other incidents is what brought me to the conclusion that Zoe was the definition of a real killer. For him, murder was second nature.

In time, I knew his whole schedule and the drop routine. I knew when the drop came in and where it came in at. I even knew where he kept his stash, but there was a speed bump. He had an eye scanner on the safe, keyed to his eye only. I spoke with Polo and Redd and we came up with a strategy for that as well. He had other stash spots, but there was no way we could hit them all. Everything was good, though. Zoe was planning a trip to Haiti, and we were set to strike soon.

———

"Hey baby."

I had just returned from making a drop for him.

"Whappun?" Zoe was laying in our king size bed.

He patted the space beside him and gestured for me to come over. I sat beside him.

"You take care of that?" he asked.

"Yea," I told him. "It's at the spot."

"That's my girl."

I kissed him and got up to go hit the shower. Under the water, I considered what was soon to come. Redd and Polo were set to come in guns blazing at 11:30. At the same time, Keisha would end Dun-Dun's life. I got out the shower, oiled myself down and put on my red bra and panties set from my Victoria's Secret collection. I looked in the mirror as I applied my red lipstick. I stepped into the bedroom to find that Zoe had gone downstairs. I looked at the clock. It was 11:17 I had less than fifteen minutes to finish up my part of the job. Setting up a romantic scene in our bedroom, I dimmed the lights and scattered rose petals all over the floor, bed and chair. If this couldn't set the mood, neither could *12 Play*.

"Zoe baby, can you come help me please?" I yelled downstairs to him. "It won't take long."

"I'm coming," he said.

He walked in and surveyed the room. "What is this?"

I approached him and sat him in the chair beside the bathroom door. I cut on some slow jams and whispered seductively in his ear.

"Just wanted to give you something to think about while you're gone."

He smiled as I started dancing for him. I swayed my hips and rocked my shit until he couldn't take the teasing anymore. I laid him back on the bed, took his clothes off and straddled him. As he eased his thick, Haitian dick inside me, I eased my hand under the pillow to grab my .38 special. I started throwing my pussy like a baseball pitcher. He gripped my ass, thrusting up into me.

"Damn mami, throw that shit!"

"Yes," I squealed. "Hit this pussy like you paying for it! Take it!"

"Ima take it," he said aggressively. "Ooh, I'ma take that shit!"

He was so into it now that his eyes were closed. I had my hand under the pillow, clutching the revolver, waiting on the signal.

BOOM!

Gunshots erupted and Zoe's eyes opened.

"What the hell is going on?"

I shot him two times in the head, spraying blood all over the pillow and bed set. I began throwing my clothes on. It sounded like Iraq downstairs. I could even hear the sounds of choppas among the gunfire. Once my clothes were on, I opened the door slowly. My nostrils were immediately filled with the smell of gunpowder. I looked down the hall and saw that someone was shooting at the crew. I crept up to him, putting the pistol to his head.

BWA!

His head exploded and his body dropped. Blood painted the wall and drenched the floor. I wiped some of the blood that had splattered my face off and made my way to Zoe's mother's room. She was desperately pushing buttons on the phone when I walked in.

"Julie!" she exclaimed. "Intruders. We must escape! Where's Zoe?"

Her eyes were a mixture of shock and confusion when I put my strap to her head. "What is the meaning of this?"

BWA!

I let my gun answer.

I came out into the hallway. Polo and Redd were running towards me with choppas.

"He's still in the room," I said. "Come on."

We ran through the hallway to Zoe's room where his body remained with his brains hanging from his head. They grabbed his body and I led them to the safe so we could grab the loot and catch out. Together they positioned his face- or what was left of it -so the eye scanner could verify his retina. The vault opened. Redd threw me two gym bags and told me to load up.

We cleaned the safe out and set the mansion on fire. No evidence. No witnesses. The way we liked it and the way it should be. Keisha was already at the hotel when we arrived. We packed our bags and checked out. We were on the next thing smokin' to College Park.

CHAPTER FOURTEEN

BALLING OUT, AINT FALLING

"*It's your fault, you killed him. If it wasn't for you he'd still be here.*"

"*No, wait. Kush, I can explain.*"

"*There's nothing left to talk about. You ruined my life!*"

"*Kush listen, it was-*"

BOOM!

I awoke in a cold sweat from the nightmare that had been keeping me up for the last two weeks. I couldn't figure it out. I'd witnessed the gruesome deaths of many. I saw things that the average female would lose her mind over. I seen people tortured right before my very eyes. But I never had nightmares. I chose this life and everything that came with it. There was no need to feel guilty. I didn't, never had and still don't. So why the midnight turmoil? Was it the fact this victim was a relative? If so, why had they begun just two weeks ago? Bear had been gone for nine months.

The digital clock on the nightstand glowed 5:43 am. To my left, Chelsea laid peacefully asleep. I had broken the news to

Violet when I got back from Florida. She took it a lot better than I thought she would. She told me she understood and she hoped we could still be friends. I was cool with that. I just hoped that Chelsea wouldn't get the idea that I was cheating. I wanted her to be able to trust me. I figured maybe we just needed to try a new environment, so we decided it was best to leave Old Nat. I bought a four-bedroom home in a neighborhood called Overlook. It seemed like a sound investment.

The lease on my Camelot apartment wasn't up when we moved, so I paid the term off to avoid fucking up my credit or making it worse than it already was. Turns out mama had been putting shit in my name for years, having already fucked up hers. I made a mental note to go check on her after I finished taking care of business. I got out of bed and headed for the bathroom. I was tired of being mad at mama. Even though she allowed my life to be the struggle it's been, I still find it hard to stay mad at her for some reason.

I tried to move around as quietly as possible as I took care of my hygiene and got ready to leave. I didn't want to wake Chelsea. She had at least another hour before it would be time for her to get ready for school. She would graduate in a week. She planned to open her own salon. Chelsea and I weren't the only ones turning up. Redd, Polo, and Keisha were doing well.

They all moved out of College Park and into Atlanta. Polo put money behind himself to start rapping. He went by Lo Dinero. With money and non-stop publicity, he was a sho-nuff success. Redd took on the trafficking trade. With Bear and the Zoepound out of the way, Redd easily maneuvered himself to the top of the totem pole. Keisha got an advisor and an accountant and invested her money in Real Estate. She had houses everywhere. She even had a stake in a few apartment complexes.

Some were low class like Old Town Villas on Godby Road. While others were high end like the one in McDonough around the corner from me called Walden Run.

I kissed Chelsea lightly on the cheek and was out the door, headed to the bank. After concluding business there I made my way to Keisha's condo. We hadn't been spending as much time together as we usually would, due to our incompatible schedules. Since Keisha had decided to leave the street life alone I hadn't had the urge to call frequently. I pulled up to the gate and waited for her to confirm me as a visitor. She buzzed me through and I pulled in. Vineyard at Maple was a really nice place to reside. The buildings were well kept, the landscape stayed fresh, and compared to what we were used to, the neighborhood was adamantly quiet. Keisha opened the door after the second knock. "What's up, girl?"

"Hey boo," I said.

"Come in, you know you don't need no invitation."

I walked inside and was taken aback by the interior decor of her pad.

"Oh my God, Keisha, who did this? I need their number, pronto."

"You already have it. Me."

"What? Are you serious?" I was truly impressed.

"Girl, you know I ain't finna let some strangers rip and run through my shit. I just had to do the best I could do. Although I did borrow a few ideas from a couple Better Home and Gardens magazines."

I looked around, taking it all in.

"I know that's right. But still, this looks really nice"

The white plush carpet complimented the zebra skin sofa set. The coffee table and two end tables were glass-top with porcelain legs. What really did the trick, was the black and white abstract painting that covered the walls.

We sat in the living room and caught up on our friendship. She filled me in on what was going on legitimately and I let her know what was poppin' in the streets. She would never relapse on her option to fall back. On top of that, I couldn't say she didn't look happy. Maybe there was hope for the fallen after all.

"So there's this guy, right?" Keisha said.

"Right."

"And I like him a lot."

"And?"

"I don't know what to say to him."

I laughed. "Keisha, we've set up some of the roughest drug dealers and you scared to talk to a nigga?"

"It's not the same," she said. "I never genuinely liked any of those guys. It was just business. It's different this time. My feelings are in this, and because of them I guess I... I just get stuck. I don't know what's wrong with me."

I turned in my seat to face her. "Okay, I'm going to pretend I'm the nigga, and you act like this is our first encounter."

She laughed. "It's gonna be easy to talk to you cause I know you."

I slapped her thigh playfully. "Girl, come on!"

"Alright, you go first."

"Hey, baby," I said with my best Barry White impression. "I got something important to tell you."

We were looking dead at each other. I rubbed the back of my fingers across her face.

"What's up?"

We gazed into each other's eyes and for some reason, a

yearning came over me. At the same time, Keisha's eyes were filled with want. Slowly, our smiles faded.

"Kush, I got something to tell you," she said.

"So... just tell me."

I could tell where this conversation was headed. Something I had been wondering for so long was finally about to be answered. I could feel it.

"I- I...,"

Before she could even answer, I leaned in and kissed her. I pulled away and we gazed into each other's eyes. Her face registered with want and confusion. For a second I thought I had crossed the line and had already begun to regret ruining our friendship. She caught me off guard when she leaned in and kissed me back. That got me horny. The feeling was serendipitous. Like a wonderful surprise by mistake. Wet with anticipation, I stuck my tongue down her throat and she released a soft moan. I was into it. Could tell she was into it, too. She pulled away.

"I'm sorry, I'm trippin'. We can't do this," she said, trying to pull herself together.

"Do what?" I said as if I didn't know.

She got up to leave but I caught her hand right before she reached the door. She wasn't about to put me out.

"Wait, where are you going?" I asked.

"I'm sorry, Kush, this ain't right. We're best friends. I don't want to fuck that up."

"We won't. I promise. We just need to get this off our chest. Don't act like the first time we kissed you didn't like it. I felt the vibe that night at Chess's house."

"Yea, but..."

"But what?"

"Our friendship is perfect," she said." Think about it, Kush. All the years we've known each other, we've never even disagreed. I don't want to lose that. Since we met we've always had each other's back. If no one else, you always knew I had you and vice versa. I just don't feel like sex is an even trade for what we've built."

I was disappointed, but I knew she was right. Keisha always had a way with words. The way she broke shit down so distinct, if I disputed any further I would come across as selfish and insensitive. The last thing I wanted to do was offend her.

I sighed. "You're right. You're absolutely right. I just got caught up in the moment, that's all. No hard feelings?"

Keisha smiled. "Never."

I convinced Keisha to chill just a little while longer. I needed to feel her out and let her know that there really was no pressure. She was like the sister I never had and I didn't want any awkwardness looming about in our future. I left Keisha's house and decided to check on mama to see how much progress she had made. I pulled into the parking lot of the rehab center, and there was barely enough space to accommodate all the visitors. Apparently, family support was a big deal to the organization. There were children, parents, grandparents, everyone. I looked into the faces of these dope fiend's relatives. They were happy, smiling even. I guess they were excited about the change they sensed was about to transpire. One long wait in line later, I finally reached the front desk.

"I'm here to see Nicole Love."

"Okay, one moment, please." The female receptionist said.

She took a look through the residence list. "I do apologize, ma'am, but it appears we do not have a resident here by that name."

"Excuse me?"

"The name, Nicole Love. There's no one here by that name."

"Well, there must be a mistake. She's been here for the last nine months. I dropped her off personally." I was genuinely confused.

The lady was beginning to look worried. "Hold on, let me make sure she's not a runaway."

"A what?"

I could feel myself growing anxious. The receptionist ignored me as she continued to scan through the list on her screen. After watching her face for the slightest signs of relief and finding none. I knew what her response would be before she lifted her head to say it.

"I'm sorry, ma'am, but according to our system, she was never here at our facility. Did you walk her in and admit her, or did you just drop her out front? Because we've had problems before where- "

I took strides towards the door as my palms grew sweaty. My emotions were a mixture of worry and fear. Was the receptionist mistaken? Or had mama never really shown up? One thing for sure, I was definitely going to get to the bottom of it.

For the rest of the day, I searched for mama until I discovered the horrific truth; she was dead. And had been for the last nine months. She overdosed on heroin the same night I dropped her off.

I'd pushed her over the edge. It was all my fault. The coroner said they had tried relentlessly to track down her loved ones but per the records, she had no one left but a daughter. When no one showed up to claim the corpse she was eventually cremated. All that was left of my family, my last remaining blood, was a vase full of ashes.

CHAPTER FIFTEEN

HUNTERS HUNTED

"**B**aby, I'm saying though," Chelsea wined.

"I don't know," I said. "I'll think about it."

Chelsea was trying to get me to go to Cali with her. She said I needed a vacation. We were in bed covered in a sheen of sweat, having just finished one of our freak sessions. In her eyes, the loss of my mother was life-changing. In mines, nothing had changed. I had been mourning the loss of my mother since I was a child. The way I saw it, mama had died a long time ago.

My phone rang and I answered it. "What up?"

"You watching the news? 'It was Redd.

"No, why?"

"Just go look," he said.

Click.

"Hello... Redd?"

My heart beat uncontrollably. The first thing that crossed my mind was that I was wanted. *FUCK*!

"Baby, what's wrong?" Chelsea asked.

I ran to the living room, cut the television on and straight to Fox 5. If I was wanted I had every intention of packing up and getting the fuck on. Chelsea came in the living room and sat on the sofa beside me.

"What's your problem?" she asked.

"Hold on," I told her. "I'm tryna see something." I turned up the volume.

"The body of twenty-three-year-old Violet Givens was discovered near a dumpster behind Kroger on Old National Highway yesterday morning. The corpse recovered was sickening. The victim's face had been lacerated so severely it was shredded beyond recognition. Forensics later found a match for the Jane Doe's dental records, identifying this unfortunate young lady."

My heart skipped a beat and my jaw dropped. I felt like a healthy woman who had just discovered she had a terminal illness. Chelsea sat beside me with her hand over her mouth in complete shock. The reporter continued.

"When asked about possible suspects, the College Park Police Department administered no comment due to the possible risk of compromising the investigation."

My phone rang again. "Hello?"

"Look at the news," Keisha said.

"Already am."

"What the fuck happened?" she yelled.

"I don't know. I haven't seen nor heard from her in weeks." I was out of it.

"Me either," Keisha said. "She stopped by my house like a week ago and that was the last time I'd heard from her."

I couldn't talk. "Keisha, let me call you back, alright?"

"Alright. Be careful, Kush. I'm serious."

"Yea."

Out of all the stories they could have been covering on the news, I would have never thought I'd see this. I could've been given a million guesses and I would have never guessed. My mind was all fucked up. Violet's death was too close to home. I never too much believed in coincidence, but if this wasn't one then that meant one of two things. Either Violet had pissed someone off, or someone was coming for me. The message was clear. My life was on the countdown.

"You alright, baby?" Chelsea tried to console me.

"Yea," I said. "I'm fine."

———

Violet's funeral was a week later at World Changes. I heard it was packed. I had planned to show face and pay my respects but for some reason, I just couldn't shake the feeling that this was somehow my fault. For the next week, I stayed in the house. I refused to go anywhere. Chelsea tried to get me out of bed but I wouldn't budge. I was so disoriented. Then Chelsea started talking about that vacation thing again.

"What's up with you and this California shit?"

"Kush, you need a break from all this- a change of scenery. Let's go on a cruise or something. You've been in the house a whole week. You haven't left or spoken to anyone. People are starting to ask questions. Come on baby, please?"

I turned over on my side and pulled the covers over my head.

Eventually, I was tired of being secluded in my room. I got up, took a shower, put on some clothes, and called Keisha to meet me at Lenox to go shopping. She was stuck showing potential home buyers several pieces of property. She promised to make it up to me next week, though. I was sure to hold her to it. I hit the mall alone and did me.

I returned home later that evening to find Chelsea had cooked dinner. Something she hadn't done in a while. She'd prepared my favorite dish. Pasta salad. After eating, I took a shower, smoked some kush and then ate again. I dozed off and was stirred awake by a noise coming from the outside of my bedroom. I clutched the pistol underneath my pillow, listening intently. I heard it again. Somebody was in my house. Hearing the same noise for the third time, I got up and crept across my bedroom floor to the door. If anyone came into my house intending to snake me in my own shit, they had another thing coming.

I opened my bedroom door slowly, trying not to make a sound. I peeped up and down the hallway. I saw no one. I heard the mysterious sound again. I got to the end of the hallway and jumped out into the living room, gun drawn and ready to blaze. To my surprise, there was no one there. I was getting frustrated. I looked down at the kitchen counter and realized the noise was just my phone. It was on vibrate. I had twenty-seven missed called from Polo. It vibrated again, and when it did, I answered.

"Yo, Lo, you know what time it is?"

"Uh, Kush, I think you need to pull up, pronto," Polo said.

"No... wait. What, why?" I asked confused and somewhat still sleep.

"Just pull up on me asap Kush, damn!" Polo lost his composure.

He had never done that before. Something was wrong. Very wrong. I tried to stay calm.

"Polo, what's going on?"

"I can't explain on the phone," he said. "Just get here as soon as you can."

"Where are you?"

"I'll text you the address. Put it in your GPS."

"Alright, I'm on my way."

I hung up the phone wondering what could be going on now. I could've sworn I heard detectives or something in the background. I hope Redd wasn't locked up. I threw on some clothes and headed for the door.

"Where are you going?" Chelsea asked groggily.

"I'm finna go meet Polo."

"This late?"

"Yes, bae. Go back to sleep."

It was 3:11 AM when I backed out of my driveway. That meant the club was still packed. Polo had invited me out to take my mind off Violet, but I had declined. If this was some half-ass scheme to get me out the house, he was in for it. Three police cruisers flew past me, sirens blaring. I could see the flashing lights spinning in the night before I reached my destination. When I pulled up there were ambulances and detectives everywhere. I saw Polo standing in a crowd of pedestrians outside the yellow crime scene tape. I parked my car, got out and approached him from behind.

I tapped him on the shoulder. "What's going on?"

He turned and I could tell he had been crying. Alarms were going off in my head. I had never seen Polo shed tears. He was fucked up. He looked as if he'd aged ten years since I last saw him. Something was up.

"Polo!" I yelled. "What the fuck is going on?"

He dropped his head and pointed. I looked and saw an irate Redd headed our way.

"Redd, what up? Why am I here?" I pointed at all the emergency response vehicles. "And what the fuck is all this shit?"

Redd shook his head then nodded towards the crime scene. "Go see for yourself."

I looked towards the crime scene, then back at Redd. My intuition was kicking in. Something was wrong. I could feel it. I almost turned around and jump back in my car. I didn't, though. I went forward, pushing through the crowd surrounding the crime scene. What took seconds felt like a mountain hike. Forensics were snapping pictures of a bloody murder scene.

The body was covered in a white sheet. I caught sight of a hand peeking from underneath. The hand was light-skinned and covered in dried blood. Yet, as visible as the red and blue lights on the roof of the police squad cars was the tattoo on the wrist. *Love's A Bitch*.

I couldn't believe it. Didn't want to believe it. Place any burden on me but please not this one. It was more than I could bear. Way more than I could stand to lose. But as much as I didn't want it to be, there was no way around it. The person under the white sheet was Keisha. All the stars that filled the night sky fell and I was shrouded in darkness. I had no family, now I had lost my best friend, too. My heart ached with a pain so excruciating I thought I would pass out. Psyched out, I stormed over to Redd and Polo. Tears were falling from my eyes uncontrollably.

"What the fuck happened to her?" I screamed.

Redd pulled his phone out, opened the gallery and handed it to me. My mouth went dry, I fell to the ground and I threw up all over the pavement. I had seen people get their eyes cut out. I had witnessed fingers being hacked off but this was worse. There was a picture of Keisha hanging from a tree with her throat slit and her tongue hanging out. When I pulled myself together Redd and Polo were beside me. I had only one question.

"Who sent it?"

"Zoepound."

———

After that day shit was never the same. Missing Keisha's funeral was a no-brainer. I hated to get emotional. Redd said to show face would be committing suicide. There was no doubt in my mind that Zoepound would be there lurking, waiting, watching my every move. I packed a few suitcases, then Chelsea and I left our house and checked into The Regency Inn. Home no longer felt safe. I put the room in a junkie's name. Anything with my name on it was fair game to be tracked. I was so fucking paranoid. Everywhere I went I felt like I was being watched. When I went out to eat I felt as though someone was there pointing and plotting.

The image of Keisha's body hanging kept popping up in my head. My dreams were replaced with nightmares and sleep was no longer a friend of mine. My mind was gone. My taste buds weren't even functioning right. Everything I put in my mouth tasted like sandpaper. I was losing weight. It got so bad that I wouldn't even leave the room unless the sun had set. I decided it was time to take Chelsea up on her offer to hit Cali. I had to get the fuck out of Georgia.

I asked Redd and Polo if they wanted to come. Polo was with it but Redd flat out bucked. He said he refused to let anybody run him out of his city. Even if it meant death. He'd take that before dishonor any day. I felt him, and it most definitely wasn't over. I just couldn't get my train of thought right long enough to come up with a plan in this environment. I needed to regroup and strategize.

The day before we left for Cali, I called Polo to make sure he was straight and ready to go. I had been calling Redd all day but I kept getting his voicemail. I hoped he was alright. Polo said he was good and was on his way to the hotel. When he arrived, we smoked and kicked it like old times. We chopped it up about what we were gonna do when we touched down in Cali.

We ran out of rellos, so we headed to the nearby liquor store. We took Polo's Escalade. He said he was going to snatch up a bottle while we were at it so he'd let me drive back, something I had been asking him to let me do since he got it. We exited the vehicle and made our way into the store. He tossed me the keys and then began searching for his poison of choice. We got what we came for and headed back to the truck. I went around to the driver's side and noticed a black Lincoln Navigator pulling up alongside. The brief distraction made me miss my footing on the curb and I dropped the keys. I opened the door and reached down to pick them up.

"Kush!" Polo shouted.

I looked up just in time to see the windows drop on the Lincoln. Mack 11's and Tech 9's popped out. I dove in the driver's seat and ducked down as shots from the automatic weapons rang out.

GLLLAOW! GLLLAOW! GLLLAOW!

Bullets ripped through the truck, shattering its windows, and glass shards rained down around me.

"Shit!" I said snatching my .45 from the small of my back.

Polo ducked down on the passenger side with his hand over the dash already bussin' back through the windshield.

"Kush!" he called. "What you doing? Drive!"

"I'm trying!" I shouted over the gunfire.

We'd backed into the parking space just in case we had to jet. Polo's truck was facing the Navi. I reached my left hand over the dash and opened fire. When the clip was empty I threw the strap out the busted driver's side window and stayed low as I crunk the truck. A new set of gunshots rang out as a second black Navi pulled into the lot. I threw the truck in drive and smashed out, swerving hard to the right and fishtailing onto 85. The black Navi's were hot on my tail. Polo returned fire, shattering the back window and causing one of the pursuing Navi's to swerve, avoiding the line of fire. I made a hard left ignoring a red light and sideswiping a navy-blue Honda. The Navi's remained in hot pursuit.

Click.

"Fuck!" Polo said.

He was out of ammo. He reached under his seat, came back up with an F&N, hit a few buttons on his radio. A hidden compartment dropped from under it containing a few extra clips.

GLLLAOW! GLLLAOW! GLLLAOW!

I tucked my head low to the steering wheel, trying my best to avoid getting hit. Barely missing a phone pole, I put the pedal to the metal and mashed as Polo popped a clip in and opened fire.

BWA! BWA! BWA! BWA!

The wind through the shattered window had my hair going wild. I had to keep using my hand to stop it from blocking my vision. Horns were blaring as I weaved in and out of traffic on the narrow two-lane road. I looked in my rearview. They weren't letting up. At the four-way, I swerved left and noticed there was blood on my hands. Frantically, I scanned my body. I knew I hadn't been hit. I hadn't felt a bullet. There was no blood on me. I hadn't even touched anything but the wheel and my hair. *MY HAIR!*

I ran my hand through my hair. There was blood, but on the right side where my head had come into contact with Polo. I glanced at Polo's side. He was hit. The blood was seeping through. I had to lose the Navi's asap so I could get him some help. I can't believe this shit! All that good policing Clayton County PD be doing and I hadn't seen not one squad car yet. I had to think of something quick. I jumped in the left lane, ignoring the upcoming and head-on traffic. I glanced in my rearview to see that one of the Navi's had done likewise, riding my bumper. The upcoming car blared its horn but I kept going flooring the accelerator. I swerved back into my rightful lane at the last minute, leaving the Navi to collide head-on with the vehicle. One down, one to go. I cut left, made a right, another left, and came out on Hawthorn.

GLLLAOW! GLLLAOW! GLLLAOW!

"Aww shit! Damn shawty!" Polo yelled, wincing in pain.

"You hit?" I asked, sounding like I was asking and telling him.

"I'm straight! Come on Kush, let's do this."

I shot a quick glance his way. I could see it in his face that he was definitely in pain. From the way his shirt looked from the side wound of his first gunshot, he was leaking profusely. I wish I could help him. I had only brought one gun with me. The Navigator picked up speed and rammed us from the back.

VUUURN-BOOM!

I lurched forward from the impact. Polo busted his nose on the dashboard. Blood trickled from my forehead from the contact with the steering wheel. I swerved a little but quickly regained control of the truck. I looked over to Polo's side mirror to see a dread head hanging out the window with long dreads flailing in the wind as he aimed.

GLLLAOW-GLLLAOW! GLLLLLAOW!

"You know what?" Polo yelled, blood spewing from his nose and mouth.

He tossed the empty clip out the window. "Fuck that. I'm done playin'. I got what they need right here."

He stuck a forty-round clip in the F&N, cocked one into the chamber, and leaned out the window.

BWA! BWA! BWA! BWA! BWA! BWA! BWA!

The dreadhead's body jerked from every shot Polo hit him with. Leaving his body dangling, before finally falling out the truck and tumbling in the street.

BWA! BWA! BWA! BWA!

Polo continued to pour his clip out as I swung left up the hill. More shooters leaned out the backseat window of the Navi.

GLLLAOW! GLLLAOW!

"Aagh, shit! What the fuck!" Polo grunted in pain.

I snatched him back in to keep him from falling. "Just sit back and let me do the rest."

Polo nodded his head vehemently as he reloaded the F&N. He was covered in blood and sweat. I had to do something fast. I hit a side street without warning. I glanced in my rearview. They were still behind us. I hit another street.

SKUURT!

I looked back again and they were still behind us. If only he could just hold off until I made it to somewhere familiar. We could jump out and get the fuck on.

"Polo, you think you might be able to run?"

No response.

"Polo?"

I looked over at him and he was staring straight ahead at nothing, head nodding. I hit his shoulder.

"Polo!"

When I tapped him, his head leaned to the side and his body slumped. I was all too familiar with death.

"Come on Polo, please," I cried. "Stay with me. We almost out of here."

I tried slapping him a couple of times on the cheek. He wouldn't budge. Polo was dead. I slammed the bottom of my fist into the steering wheel.

"Fuck!"

I was furious. I grabbed the F&N out of Polo's hand as I flew across 138. The Navi was gaining on me. If nothing else, one thing was clear. They were determined to make this my last night on Earth. The problem with that was that I had already made up my mind the exact opposite. I dug my hand into my armrest and grabbed my knife.

VUUUR-BOOM!

They rammed me from behind again. I sped up and bent the next corner, a street familiar to me. I put the knife in my pocket and hopped out the Escalade, sending it flying through some-one's garage.

GLLLAOW! GLLLAOW!

They continued to shoot at me as I ran for my life.

GLLLAOW! GLLLAOW! GLLLAOW!

I felt a sharp pain in my shoulder and I knew I was hit. I would never forget the feeling of a bullet lodged in my flesh. I sucked it up and kept pushing. There was a fence up ahead. I jumped it and kept running, moving so fast I stumbled. There was no one behind me, yet my flight instinct had kicked in and I couldn't stop running if I wanted to. I saw a bando up ahead. Tonight, however, it seemed a haven. I hopped the fence to the backyard and kicked in the backdoor. I tried my best to make the door look closed, then I peeped out the blinds to see if anyone had seen me enter. I put my back against the wall and slid to the floor.

"Fuck!" I said.

My chest heaved as I tried to catch my breath.

How did they know where to find me? I had just left the hotel five or ten minutes prior. I hadn't even been on the scene long. They must've already been following Polo but didn't know he was at the Regency Inn to fuck with me. Okay, but how did they get Redd's number to send a picture? Why even look for him or Polo in the first place? As far as Zoepound knew, they had been infiltrated and robbed by two women. Violet's death was more confusing. She had never stepped foot in Florida and we hadn't been hanging out like that. Killing her would be insignificant to me. It just didn't add up. There were more holes in this mystery than the George Zimmerman and Casey Anthony trials combined. I patted my pockets for my phone. I needed Chelsea or Redd to come pick me up but that was dead because my phone was still in Polo's Escalade on the charger.

My shoulder throbbed like an inflated bruise, causing me to bite down and clenched my eyes shut as I held my arm and withered in pain. I dreaded what I was about to do next but I had to stop the bleeding.

I took the knife out my pocket and cut the same hair that I had always cherished. I didn't give a damn about no hair. I was lucky to be alive. The only people who survived shit like that was Tom Cruise and Jackie Chan. I hacked my hair down to a little past my earlobes. I attempted to remove my shirt but was halted by the excruciating pain in my shoulder. I cut it down the middle of the front, took it off as carefully as I could, and put my shirt in my mouth trying to muffle my screams. I bit down like a rave dancer on the molly. I brought the knife to my shoulder wound and I dug the bullet out so I could begin to heal. Thick, dark crimson blood poured from my shoulder. I tied one half of my shirt around my shoulder to stop the bleeding. With the other half, I made a sling to relieve the pressure in my collarbone.

For some reason, I still didn't feel safe. I crawled to the opposite side of the living room and sat upright against the wall, facing the door with the F&N in hand and finger on the trigger. I took a deep breath on high alert in nothing but shoes, jeans, and a bra. I was beyond paranoid and my trigger finger itched. I craved blood. Nothing would please me more than to drench the soil with the blood of my enemies. I was psyched out. If anyone came through that door, Zoepound or not, it would be the last threshold they would ever cross. I was in a fucked-up mood. First Violet, then Keisha, and now Polo. Oh, this wasn't over by a long shot. I had every intention of getting to the bottom of this. When I did, I was gonna make some noise about it.

I sat on the floor for hours just watching the door and trying to piece this puzzle together. But that was no easy task when you couldn't figure out the missing pieces. I racked my brain about what we could have possibly left behind or maybe had said to Zoepound for them to know where to find us. One thing was certain, the vacation was canceled. Fuck Cali. Whoever was after me had taken the lives of three people close to me. I wasn't going nowhere. Retribution was a must, even if it took my last breath in the process.

CHAPTER SIXTEEN

PAYBACK FROM WAYBACK

I stayed in the bando for two days without food, water or a shower before I finally decided it was time to take action. I upped the F&N on an unsuspecting neighbor and threw her in the trunk of her silver Infinite after taking her shirt and cellphone. I had so much to do with so little time to spare. I tried calling Redd to no avail. He didn't answer. As far as I knew, he was the only one left. But after several calls and no answer, I was starting to think he was dead. Shit had got real fast.

I could think of only one person who could help me. An old friend. First, there was someone else I needed to talk to. I pulled into the cemetery and drove around to my father's lot. I got out and went the rest of the way on foot. As I passed a hedge with roses, I plucked one for my daddy and continued on my way until I came to his tombstone.

Richard "Rich" Love.

"Hey daddy," I said. "How have you been? It's been a while,

huh? I know. I know you're mad about the way things have been going but don't worry. I plan on handling it real soon. I'ma make you proud. Mama checked out on me since my last visit, but I'm sure you know about that...."

I stood above daddy's grave trying to figure out what more to say. All around me were tombstones as far as the eye could see. It was crazy how many people were dead in just this small speck of land. It was crazy how much I'd contributed to the graveyard in my short life and how much more I intended to contribute to avenge my crew by any means.

"I avenged you daddy. I caught up with Junior so you can rest in peace knowing the person responsible has met his doom, at the hand of your daughter at that."

I could feel myself getting emotional but I didn't want to cry. All my problems were still at an all-time high. Despite the fact, I couldn't stop.

"Walk with me, daddy. You gotta have my back like you said you would." Sobs racked my body and tears slid down my face. "I need you, daddy. You said you'd always be there for me. But they took you... they took you away from me." I let the tears fall, getting everything off my chest. Then I wiped my eyes and tightened up.

"I miss you daddy. I love you, bye."

I dropped the rose by his tombstone and headed to the road. Up ahead, a family was just exiting a pearl black Toyota Corolla.

———

"Kush," Fuwah greeted me with a big hug. "It's been a very long time, my friend."

We were in an abandoned gas station across the street from the Shell. I still had the cellphone of the unsuspecting neighbor from earlier but her car was another story. I had been texting Redd from her phone all day wanting to meet up with him to brief him on the recent mishaps and discuss our get back before I met up with Fuwah, but he still wasn't responding.

"I know, glad to see you too, Fuwah."

He looked at my arm. "What is this?"

I shrugged. "Trouble follows me, I guess."

"Yes, yes. I've heard. Big trouble.

"So, tell me what you know," I said.

There was a nice chunk of money being offered to anyone with information of my whereabouts. Hearing my name, Fuwah feigned interest and was given an address to meet for his proposition. He sent one of his men from the UFO in his place and discovered they were Haitians, Zoepound to be exact. His henchman spoke to someone who was said to have just taken over due to the former leader's unfortunate end. After hearing all the details, he left, telling them that he would be in touch, but he'd never called back. He'd heard all he needed to hear.

"Did you happened to catch his name?" I asked. "This guy you spoke with."

"Ummm, Doe-Doe, Dae-Dae. Something like that, yes."

Didn't ring a bell. "No, can't say I know him. Did you bring the arsenal I requested?"

He reached behind a safe and pulled out a duffle bag. "Why yes. Of course, my friend."

He unzipped the bag and began pulling out the arsenal. Two Smith and Wesson .45's with an extended clip holding thirty hollow tips. I was on my one shot one kill shit. As a bonus, I was given two extra extended clips loaded with hollows. I couldn't be caught out in the water like last time. I needed ammunition. Included were four hand grenades, a Mac 10 and a silencer. I tried not to overdo it considering I could only use my right arm as it is. I could move my left to aim and shoot but it would take tremendous effort. After all, it wasn't my arm that had taken the bullet. It was my shoulder. I figured if I bent my arm at the elbow I could aim with my forearm alone. He loaded everything back in the bag and handed it over.

The stolen phone vibrated in my pocket. I pulled it out and there was a text from a number I didn't recognize.

Unknown Number:
Meet me at the old hideout

That could only be one person.

"Thanks, Fuwah. I owe you for life. You may have just saved mine." I headed for the exit.

"Kush?" Fuwah called just before I made it to the back door.

I looked over my shoulder. "Yea, what up?"

His face was grim. "The Haitians are ruthless. They won't stop until you're six feet in the ground. Be careful."

―――

I pulled into Hillandale right after sunset. Everything looked the same except for the lack of people outside. Hillandale used to always be live. No matter what time of day or night there was something to get into. It was a different story now. Those were the days of the 90's baby. This new generation was too busy being pacified by electronics. I rode past the old group home shaking my head. 2013 had been one hell of a year. I parked the car and headed to the cut that was once a secret hideout. Other than the new twigs, vines and bushes that had grown in our absence, it pretty much seemed untouched. Like no one else had even discovered it. One more indication that kids weren't exploring their neighborhoods like they used to. When I reached the heart of the hideout, I saw Redd and immediately embraced him. I thought I'd never see him again.

"What happened to your hair?" he asked. "No, wait... I know. Polo."

"How?" I asked.

"The news. His and your face have been all over the news for the last few days," he said solemnly.

I wonder why Fuwah failed to mention that to me. Or if he even knew. "Well, where have you been?" I asked. "I was beginning to think you were dead."

Redd smiled a rare smile. "Naw, I had to regroup and check something out real quick. They said your phone was found on the scene. Wasn't no tellin' whose number you had programmed or what messages you didn't delete. When I started receiving the text messages from you earlier, I thought someone was fishing. Then I got the hideout idea and thought to set a trap before it hit me that we were the only two who knew about this spot. I figured if it was you, you would show. If not, I would just go ahead and change my number on the strength."

I nodded.

"And if a nigga tried to kill me you would have heard about it on the news," Redd said. "Cause before I die, I'm taking half of them with me"

It was my turn to smile. "I'm going after them. You were right. I ain't lettin' no damn nobody run me out of my city. I'm bringing the fight to their doorstep. Ima get something for that shit. For Violet, Polo, and for Keisha! So you down or what?"

"Hell yea I'm down! There's something else that needs handling first, though."

"Something like what?" I asked, confused. For the life of me, I couldn't think of anything more pressing at the moment.

Redd had his poker face on. "The real reason I closed camp and called you here is that a question that was once a mystery is clear now."

I was still lost. "What mystery, Redd? You're not making any sense."

He looked me dead in my eyes. "I know who's been feeding Zoepound intel on us."

I seriously wanted to know this. "Who?"

"Think about it," he said. "You're smart. Read between the lines. The person is the only living individual with personal ties to the crew. The only person who knows who we are, where we're from and what we're capable of. So I'ma kick it to you like this; either you handle it or I will. As for Zoepound, we'll handle them together then we move on with our lives. You got two days, Kush. I love you." He kissed me on my forehead. "Ima call you in two days, aiight?"

I was stuck. I knew who he was insinuating. It was obvious as a red Kool-Aid stain on a white suit. I just didn't want to believe it. It didn't make sense. Being real with myself it was hard to pinpoint any one specific person when we'd slimed so many people.

I was on some real fuck it type shit, so I decided to head home for the night. To my surprise, Chelsea was there, she opened the door and she hugged me with a similar embrace that I'd given Redd. I took a shower, made sure the house alarm was secure and then cuddled with Chelsea with both my .45's under my pillow. All through the night, Redd's words replayed in my head. *"This person is the only living individual with personal ties to the crew...."*

The next morning I woke up to Chelsea screaming. I grabbed both my straps and ran to the living room. Chelsea had her hands over her mouth, staring at the television. I walked around the sectional and fixed my eyes on the screen to see that the news was on.

"Twenty-four-year-old Raphael Hicks shot seven times with an assault rifle."

"What the fuck!" I yelled. "I was just with him yesterday."

Chelsea shot me a look.

"...think this murder is somehow linked to the bloodshed that has recently erupted throughout the city..." the reporter continued.

This had to be a nightmare I couldn't wake up from. There on the scene were the faces that made up the crew. Polo, Redd, Keisha and mine. They even had Violet's picture. That didn't make sense. The murders had different styles and motives. Somebody was talking. Not just to Zoepound, but the police. As far as the authorities knew, I was still alive and still at large and they were now offering a handsome amount for my whereabouts. All they wanted was information that led to my capture. It was all just an 1800-CRIME STOPPER phone away.

That was it! Zoepound had to go. It was either them or me. Kill or be killed. I wasn't going anywhere. I refused. For the rest of the day, I sat in my room thinking about what Redd had told me last night. I pondered about what he had told me throughout our years rocking together, trying to make sense of things. He had been killed at his own crib. I didn't even know where he lived. This crazy because it only reiterated. No one was to be trusted. NOT ONE SOUL.

I found myself crying again. I've done more crying in the last month than I'd done most of my life. I had to let out the hurt, loss and pain for my fallen friends. For Violet, Keisha, Polo.... and now Redd. I watched Chelsea as she made dinner that night, wondering if she could be trusted. She had set me up once before so it wasn't beyond her and I definitely wasn't putting it past her, but everything in me screamed to give her the benefit of doubt.

———

I woke up around 12:30 am and threw on my all black trap suit. I grabbed my Nike knapsack. In it, I threw four grenades and the two .45's. I put the extenders in my pocket. They were originally for Redd but that was no longer an option. By myself that was too many guns. It was bad enough that I would barely be able to hold one. Despite the fact, I was about to go cannon. I half didn't expect to make it back. Why would it matter? I had no friends or family to return to. They were all where I would be if I didn't make it- on the other side. Chelsea stirred and I realized the foolishness of my thoughts as I watched her sleep peacefully. She was everything to me. I look down at the address on the piece of paper Fuwah had given me. It was a Fayetteville address to a Dix-lee-on neighborhood. I looked back down at Chelsea. Then I leaned down and kissed her forehead.

I went outside to start up the Corolla that I'd stolen from the cemetery from the family visiting the gravesites. I put the car in drive and pulled out of the driveway having backed in just in case I had to make a speedy getaway. I looked back at our house one more time and could've sworn I saw the curtain move. I shook it off and kept going. No more distractions. I needed this taken care of so I could move on with my life. *It was probably just Chelsea.*

I rode around the neighborhood looking for a mailbox with the numbers 300 on it. The house wasn't as big as Zoe's was in Miami. The neighborhood was a big ass circle. I was looking for possible escape routes and checking the area for police like Redd had taught me. I parked down the street from the Zoepound HQ house and got out on foot. I crept back down the street to the house and walked the perimeter to get a feel of things before I went Rambo or in my case, Kill Bill. I went back around to the front. On me, I had two .45's, four grenades and two extra clips. Fuck it. Let retribution begin. I pulled two grenades out and said a silent prayer. OV.

I snatched the pin out the grenades and threw one through a downstairs window and one through an upstairs window then waited.

"What the fuck!" I heard someone shout.

"Oh, shit!" Dun- "

BOOM! BOOM!

Whatever he was about to say was cut short by the explosions. I moved quickly and swiftly with the intent to kill any and everything that moved. I kicked in the front door and rushed through the house. I wasn't alone. With me was the element of surprise. Smoke, dust and debris filled the air. Little fires had started in isolated areas. Lifeless and disoriented bodies lay sprawled about the living room. Some were females who looked to have been in the middle of sexual intercourse when the grenades had gone off.

BWA! BWA! BWA!

I left holes in they asses for good measures.

BWA! BWA!

No love. All I see is red.

BWA!

I rounded the corner to go up the stairs and finish whoever was up there before they could get right. I hit the first step and jump back behind the wall just in time.

BOP-BOP-BOP-BOP-BOP!

"Stupid bitch!" one of the Hattians yelled at me. "I fuckin' murder you!"

"I got yo bitch," I said as I pulled the pin from another grenade and launched it up the steps.

"You hear me! I- "

BOOM!

He was cut short by the blast. His body landed right in front of me.

BWA! BWA!

I finished him. "Who's the bitch now?" I said to his corpse.

"Aww shit! "

I heard moans of agony from upstairs and headed in that direction. At the top, I found three Haitians laid out in the hall-way. One's brains decorated the wall, one was fighting to stay conscious with shrapnel stuck in the left side of his face and the other was missing his whole forearm.

BWA! BWA! BWA!

I blasted the one with the shrapnel. The one with the missing forearm was in so much agony he paid me no mind, he looked familiar. I kicked him in his ribs, rolling him over onto his back. It was B-Style, the Zoepound affiliate who had killed the prospect for returning from his initiation without emptying the entire clip.

"Fuck you!" He spat blood at me.

"Nigga fuck with me!" I spat back with a round between his eyes.

BWA!

I moved stealthily down the hall with my back on the wall, trying to stay focus.

"Kuuush!"

Someone yelled out from one of the rooms on the far side of the hall. I waited in silence. Maybe I was trippin'.

"Kuuush!" they yelled. "I know it's you! Show yourself, you cutthroat bitch! You heartless-evil-deceitful bitch!"

The voice was coming from the room that I'd thrown the second grenade into. Pistol in front of me, I inched my way down the hall to see who it was. Who had been expecting me? I stepped through the doorframe. The bed was flipped over. There was money all over the floor and a fire had begun to spread by the bookshelf near the entrance to the bathroom. The window was completely blown out. The sounds of sirens off in the distance met my ears but I could care less. I wasn't leaving until every son of a bitch in this motherfucker was breathless.

"Well done Julie, or shall I say... Kush?" a familiar voice said in broken English.

I couldn't believe my eyes. This was getting more confusing by the second. Sitting up against the wall, legs gone from mid-thigh down was Dun-Dun. He must've been counting money right before the grenade flew through the window and into his lap. The sight was ugly. But what had been done to my friends was much more horrendous.

"What the fuck you still doing alive?" I said with my gun trained on him.

"I could ask you da same t'ing," he chuckled. "What? Not happy to see me?"

A cigarette rested near what was left of his leg. He picked it up and lit it using the fire that had begun to spread. The sirens were getting closer.

"You killed Keisha," I said.

"You murdered Zoe," he said. "After you deceived him into believing you actually understood and cared for him. He fucked with you and you spat in his face."

"Fuck Zoe!"

"No, bitch, fuck you, you hear me? Fuck you witta horse dick, you fucking animal! You took away da closet t'ing I had to family, all that I had left. You tried to kill me too but you failed. You're a fucking failure!"

BWA!

I shot him in the shoulder.

"Ahh!" he screamed, spitting blood as sweat super soaked his body.

"That's for my shoulder, you no-dick bastard."

He started laughing. "You t'ink you can hurt me? Is that what you t'ink? Well, let me tell you something. I have nothing to lose. There's nothing left for me in this world. My heart bleeds for you alone right now. I've enjoyed making your life a living hell these pasts months."

BWA!

I shot him in the right shoulder and he laughed like the Joker himself. Sweat pouring from his head. He was drenched. "How the fuck did you survive?" I yelled.

"Wouldn't you want to know," he laughed some more. "Okay,

I'll tell you eeeveryting." The hysterical laughter started then subsided. "Mona," Dun-Dun explained. "Or Keisha, shot me eleven times. Thought I was a goner but I'm strong like a lion. She plan to torch di place but, my people got to me before she could set the fire. They found me and got help. We found about Zoe too late, but it was clear that y'all was in cahoots and it was set up all di while." He paused to take a pull from the cigarette. He exhaled and continued. "I had my room dusted for prints. I send dem to a friend in forensics. Luckily that bitch of a friend of yours had a record. Keisha Stockham. College Park, Georgia. I arrived and began watching her. Just as I thought. The two of you were together shopping, buying houses and just splurging like you earned it."

"We did," I defended.

"You stole it!" he protested.

"And what did y'all do for a living, huh? I was there Dun-Dun I know what's goin' on. Your crew was no different from mine. Same shit, different toilet bowl."

"Whatever." He hit the cigarette again and spat. "It doesn't matter now, anyway. You know how the story ends. I accept my fate. As for you, you're a dead bitch walking. I don't know how you managed to make it this far but in the end, you'll get back what you put out. Be careful who you say you love."

"What about everyone else?" I wanted to know.

He shook his head. "I'll say this and then I have to leave."

He had to be seriously delirious. Where the fuck did he think he was finna go?

"Karma has always been a bitch. That's one woman who will never change. You'll get your bite in the ass soon enough, you manipulative bitch! Your past will come for you, along with the deeds and unfinished business of betrayal."

He was laughing again, more maniacal than before, and it was starting to piss me off.

"Your time has come," he said between fits of laughter. "Kiss my fiancée for me."

He reached behind himself and before I could even move my finger to let off a shot, he put the pistol to his head and pulled the trigger.

CHAPTER SEVENTEEN

KARMA'S A BITCH

Lightning flashed, thunder boomed and heavy rain pelted the top of the stolen Corolla as I made my way home. Feeling like time was working against me, I pushed the gas way past the speed limit, throwing caution to the wind. I was in a lot of pain. The adrenaline rush from the mission had subsided and the wear and tear on my shoulder was catching up with me. There was no time to acknowledge the pain, though. More imperative issues were in mind. Like why Keisha hadn't told us about the unexpected visit that caused her not to eradicate all traces left by the crew. We could have done damage control before things had gotten this far. Everyone is dead now. No wonder Keisha had backed out of the streets to go legit. She was running from her past, her karma. Yet it found her- her, Redd and Polo -and there was still a loose end unattended. A loose end with answers to all my remaining questions. Answers that would create new problems as well.

Seeing Dun-Dun again reminded me just how small this

world really is. It also reiterated the fact that anything was possible and to expect the unexpected. I remember what Keisha disclosed about Dun-Dun, it confirmed my suspicions and broke my heart at the same time. I thought about the first time I linked up with Chelsea at the club. She had mentioned relocating to Miami. I thought about the first time I invited her to my apartment in Camelot. She was wearing a South Beach T-shirt. I thought about all the trips to Florida and back that she mentioned her fiancé took. The proof was in the pudding and Dun-Dun's comment was confirmation. He was her fiancé. Chelsea was the informant.

I sat in the car trying to fix myself up in an attempt to stop the pain, physical and emotional. It was 4 AM. I grabbed my strap from the passenger seat, knowing what I had to do but I couldn't see myself going through with it. My life was damaged beyond repair. Chelsea was the single thread that held it together. Without her, my whole world would fall apart. What was the point in having money with no one to share it with? No one from the bottom to look back with from the top? I'd spend the rest of my life in question, wondering if the people around me loved me for me, or simply for what I could do for them. That was no way for a woman to live.

I put the pistol down and got out of the car. I looked at the bloodstained driver's seat before closing the door. Maybe there was more to it. I needed to hear her side of the story. I was sure she could explain. It wasn't fair of me to jump to conclusions. Walking in the house, I locked the door behind me and attempted to turn on the lights in the living room. When they didn't come on, I looked up at the chandelier and flicked the switched vigorously. Then came a snivel.

"They're not gonna come on, Kush."

I turned around to find Chelsea sitting on the couch, holding a revolver. Tears began to fall from my eyes, mixing with the raindrops on my face. I was hurt, but in no way surprised. I just had one question.

"Why?" I whispered. "I went against everything for you."

With the gun trained on me, she wiped her eyes with the back of her free hand.

"It wasn't supposed to end like this. You should've just came to Cali with me when I asked."

I shook my head in disbelief and ran my hands through my soaked hair, eyes clenched tight. Maybe, just maybe, if I clenched them tight enough, my problems would fade away when I opened them. But that wasn't happening, though.

"Chelsea, tell me... "

She dropped her head, still maintaining her aim.

"Not too long after you came back from Florida, Redd put a pistol to my head and threatened to kill me if I didn't stop seeing you. He hated the fact that you forgave me and that you cared about me so much. In his eyes, I would be your downfall. No stranger to Redd and his outdated scare tactics, I took it in stride. Then he told me about you and Keisha. At first, I shook that off but the doubt kicked in. You've cheated before so I couldn't be sure. I don't think you understand how heart broke I really was."

She looked as if she expected a response. I started to defend myself against the lie Redd had told but changed my mind. No sense beating a dead horse. I wondered how someone who claimed to love you could be so easily manipulated into doubting your faithfulness.

"A week later I got a call from my ex-fiancé."

"Dun-Dun?" I asked.

She nodded solemnly, diverting her eyes.

"He said he was in town and wanted to speak with me. We met and he told me that he'd recently been shot eleven times by a woman who stole his heart after I called off the marriage. When I asked how his family was doing he said they were fine and in a much better place. He said his visit was to thank the woman responsible. He went on to say that since he'd been following his ex-lover, that her trail led him straight to the other woman responsible, just as expected. What wasn't expected, was that I had any connection with them. I had no idea what was going on but when he showed me the pictures of you, him, Zoe and Keisha in Florida but I was able to put the pieces together. Your lengthy disappearances, the random trips you would take all made sense. He wanted you and Keisha dead, but for me, this was a chance to get rid of Redd. So, I told him about your crew."

I cut her off. "No Chelsea. What were you thinking?"

With each sentence she spoke, the events that led to my crews' demise were made clear.

"He wanted revenge!" she cried out. "And I wanted us to be together so I made a deal. I told him what he needed to know to eliminate your crew. In return, he agreed to let you live. Your punishment would be to live with no one to love, except for me of course. So, I gave up Violet as well. Once I gave him the information he needed, he told me to take you and get the hell out of Georgia because things were about to get ugly... but you wouldn't come and one by one your friends began to fall until you agreed. Sometime during our absence, Polo would get him, but you invited him and ruined everything! If he fled as well, Dun-Dun would've assumed foul play. I couldn't take that chance."

Slowly she stood and approached me even slower, bringing

the gap between us to point-blank range. She couldn't even look me in my eyes. I knew what was next.

"You threw me to the wolves, didn't you?" I said. "You leaked on me and Polo the night we left The Regency."

I took a step back and my eyes narrowed from the disgust towards the very person that only hours ago symbolized my will to go on. The illuminated insidiousness once concealed in a gray cloud of deception began to stir within me a feeling far deeper than words.

"Love...." I said.

And what began as an unconscious statement ended intro-spectively. "Who would've guessed that embracing it would camouflage the thin line isolating hate?"

"He lied to me, though. He promised me your life in exchange for closure."

She sounded so helpless I almost felt sorry for her.

"I couldn't stand to lose you again by any means. I- I got desperate and spoke to a detective the morning after the night of Polo's death. I wanted you out of harm's way. He told me to give him a call if I spotted you, but before I could bring myself to turn you in, Redd was murdered this morning and you decided to play for keeps."

She paused and I stared into her eyes as she nodded, her gaze so strong. She looked as though she was staring through me. Her face wore the expression of someone whose luck somehow seems to get worse no matter how she rolled the dice, the expression of someone who had gambled with no conscious and had lost it all. The hopeless look in her distant gaze told the story of the moment she realized she had just pulled her last card with no change in fortune.

Her voice was barely above a whisper. "I knew if you managed to survive, you'd discover my part in this, this... "

"Scheme."

"No!" she snapped.

Then just as suddenly her voice was the unmistakable tone of finality.

"I mean, it wasn't supposed to be... I did this for us, but he used me. I love you so much I just... By the time I figured out Dun-Dun's true intentions, I was in too deep. I had gone too far to go back and now- now you see me as a loose end."

For the first time in my life, I was at a complete loss for words. Somehow appalled just didn't cut it. Even worse was that I could see that she truly believed she was without fault. For love, she said, but I couldn't see it. And if in some crazy, twisted sort of way she did love me, then with lovers like that who had room for enemies? If in any way that was love, then the world could feel free to hate me. I could tolerate hate, but a broken heart is an indescribable feeling.

Love is a double edge sword with one hell of a blacksmith. In the beginning, it makes the heart beat with a rhythm so euphoric, like unknowingly ingesting some fascinating new strain of cannabis. And on the other blade, the edge is so sharp that the wounds are subject to leave you suicidal.

Like now, where most would beg for their lives, I stood waiting for the bullet that would end it all, welcoming it. The absence of love and genuine authenticity made living life useless. What would I live for? I'd only be waiting for her to cross me again. If not her, then someone else. Because if my real enemies didn't get me, my fake friends certainly would. So, fuck it. I'm tired anyway. Tired of watching out for all the people I'd wronged. Tired of tossing and turning, wondering if I had somehow slipped along the way and was now on the run. Twenty-one years young and my whole life has been nothing but heartache and pain. Since eighteen, I've wanted for nothing. But the good times were haunted by the shadows of what was yet to come. Chelsea pointed the gun at my chest.

"I wish I could let you live. I love you so much. I just- I wish none of this year ever happened. But if I don't kill you, I know you're going to kill me."

I fell to my knees. I embraced death wholeheartedly. I now understood how Dun-Dun must've felt in the final seconds of his existence. Thanks to ambition and greed, he no longer perceived life as life, let alone a life worth living. Like Dun-Dun, I accepted my fate all the same. *"Be careful who you say you love."* Dun-Dun had said. He'd learned from loving Keisha and now I knew from loving Chelsea. He knew personally that this would hurt more than any bullet he had with my name on it. Which is why I am still here. I dropped my head at the irony, how sinister. Chelsea sniveled and wiped the tears from her face with the back of her free hand once again.

"I love you, Kush."

BOOM!

CHAPTER EIGHTEEN

TO LIVE WITH NO ONE TO LOVE

I sat on the far side of the crowded Greyhound bus station watching the news in disbelief. Not because I was on Georgia's Most Wanted list, but because Redds's mugshot was right beside mines. The white man with the sandy brown hair looked serious as he gave the details on Redd.

"...the body believed to be Raphael Hicks was not him, but someone else. Police officials say dental records of the John Doe did not match up with the records they have on file for Hicks," the news anchor said.

I was watching this for the second time since seeing it at Fuwah's house earlier, but that didn't make it any easier to wrap my mind around. Redd had faked his death. But where was he now? Why hadn't he reached out to me?

A white man walked past me and I pulled the baseball cap lower on my head. I didn't want him to notice my scars. I was a nervous wreck, even with Fuwah's tall, dark skin, gorilla looking Muslim brother Faheem watching over me from the front door.

Fuwah was in line getting my tickets we pre-ordered online. It was the only way to get a bus ticket without an I.D. Life in Georgia had become a threat to my freedom. So I was leaving to start a new life in Spokane, Washington. I had no idea why the particular location but Fuwah insisted so I agreed. All we were waiting, for now, was for Fuwah's contact to get here with my document. Then I was out of here for good. I wasn't looking forward to the three days and fourteen hours ride, but I came too far to spend the rest of my life locked up for murder. Besides, there was nothing left for me here anyway. Last night I watched the love of my life blow her brains out right before my eyes, killing herself and my final reason for being. I guess in her own way that I'll never understand, Chelsea really did love me.

Fuwah made it to the front of the line and was talking to the Greyhound rep when Big Rod walked in the station's entrance and made his way to the vending machines. Instinctively I reached for the small of my back but nothing was there. I began to panic. Big Rod had seemed straight but either this was the world's greatest coincidence or he was here on a mission. I shot a nervous glance from Fuwah to Faheem, both seemingly oblivious to the enemy at hand. I looked back to the vending machine and he was gone. I looked left and right, senses on alert. A baby started crying somewhere in the station. My heart started racing as the Pacman and Galaga arcade quarter machines seemed louder all of a sudden. Where had he gone so fast

There was a tap on my shoulder, and I jumped and turned to find Big Rod standing behind me.

"Richelle, bout time I found you." He reached behind himself. "I been lookin' all over for you."

"Wait!" I stood and put my hands out. People were looking our way. "You don't have to do this."

Big Rod paused with his hand behind his back looking confused. "Do what?"

He pulled out a small manila envelope and handed it to me. I opened it and pulled out an I.D, driver's license, passport and birth certificate with my picture but the name Ke'Asia Leonard on it.

It was my turn to be confused. "Wait... you're -"

"Ah, Big Rod," I turned to see Fuwah and Faheem walking up. "Nice of you to finally join us, my friend."

"Friend?" I looked from Fuwah to Big Rod. I was really lost, now. "You two... know each other?"

Fuwah smiled. "Indeed. He is my contact."

"But how?"

"He's the one responsible for the money I was paid to watch over the house for you all those years," Big Rod said.

I looked to Fuwah for confirmation. "Is this true?"

"Yes."

"But why? You knew my Dad?"

"I didn't, but my Muslim brother did."

I looked at Faheem.

"No, no, not Faheem. Qawi."

"Khi-who?"

"Daddyo," Big Rod said. "Qawi is his Muslim attribute. Back before he took his Shahada he went by the name Daddyo, and he was a part of our crew. It was me, your father, your uncle Rod, Daddyo, and two women. We worked for-"

Fuwah put his hand up. "That is enough, Big Rod. Kush, take this, my friend."

He handed me my bus ticket and some more money that I really didn't need.

"But what about clothes and stuff. And why Spokane, Washington? Who's out there? Why not send me to this Daddyo person? Where is he? I want to talk to him."

The overhead intercom came on. "All passengers boarding the bus to Spokane, Washington head to the bus lane at this time."

"Come now, Kush." Fuwah put his hand on my shoulder and guided me to the bus lane with Big Rod and Faheem following close behind. "You can speak to him when you get there?"

"That's -"

"Where you're going. Yes, of course."

We weaved in and out of the crowd while Big Rod and Faheem struggled to keep up. I couldn't believe how packed it was for a bus ride to Spokane. Before this morning, I had never heard of it. We got to the bus and stopped just outside of it.

Fuwah put both his hands on either side of my shoulders. "Listen, my friend. You are to use the money I gave you to buy clothes once your bus makes a stop in Texas. You will pass through there on your way to Washington. You will be a good distance from here by then. I do not want to risk taking you shopping now. Not here. Your face is being shown everywhere. I know you have sustained a significant financial loss due to what you must leave behind, but it is for the better. I have contacts who may be able to help me recover some of it but most of it will be lost, I am afraid."

He hugged me for the first time, and when he pulled back, his eyes were moist. "It saddens me to see you go, but it is best. I fear of what you may discover about your past when you arrive but you need to know."

My brows creased in confusion. "Know what?"

"Sorry, Kush. But it isn't my place to tell you that."

Big Rod walked up and tried to lift me, but couldn't. I cringed from the pain and soreness.

"Guess you done got too big to lift up and spin around."

They laughed, and for the first time in weeks, I smiled. The memory took me back to a time when things were simple.

Then Big Rod did something he hadn't done in fifteen years. He hugged me. I was shocked at first, then I hugged him back.

"There's a letter at the bottom of the envelope," Big Rod whispered. He pulled back and smiled. "Take care of yourself, Richelle."

I nodded. "You know I will."

I said my last farewells and boarded the bus, thinking about how wild my twenty-four years on this Earth had been. My whole life had been spent in College Park and the streets of Atlanta. And as I stared at the city outside my window, I didn't know how I felt about leaving it all behind. What's more is I didn't know if I'd ever return, or if I ever could.

EPILOGUE

Dear Diary,
      Today is the first day of the year 2015, and I've decided to keep this diary to help make sense of all the thoughts in my head.

It's been a little over a year since I witnessed Chelsea shoot herself in our living room, made Georgia's Most Wanted list, and relocated to Spokane, Washington.

I think about my friends and all the things I left behind, and though it hurts, I smile to myself sometimes thinking about what Polo and Keisha would say if they knew I was working at a post office. Lol! They would never let me live it down.

I miss them so much. Smh. Redd and Chelsea, too.

Qawi's been great. He got me this job. And though I'm not exactly making the best money, it does feel good to live a normal life for once. No dodging police. No looking over my shoulders for enemies. No penitentiary chances or risking my life for my next check. None of that. But the nightmares were another story altogether. They had gotten worse. Particularly the one about my uncle.

The letter Big Rod left at the bottom of my envelope revealed daddy's true killer. It wasn't my uncle. It was Jamaica Ray. My Daddy's crew worked for him for a little over a year, and rose to the top but as Daddy's clientele grew Jamaica Ray began to see him as a threat and started cutting his product. He even went as far as having their spots robbed, their workers slaughtered and still made them pay for the work. I couldn't believe it. Redd's father was my daddy's murderer. The "JR" on the envelope I found never meant Junior. It wasn't an abbreviation. They were initials. Jamaica Ray. I didn't know how to feel about the whole thing. It was one thing to kill an uncle you never knew for the treachery he committed, but could I kill my best friend about something his father was responsible for? Sometimes I wonder if Redd ever knew. Was he as in the blind as I was about the whole thing? Does it even matter? I wasn't sure. The only thing I did know was that this was a small world. And that as sure as the sky was blue, I'd see him again.

One day...

BOOKS BY URBAN AINT DEAD'S C.E.O

Elijah R. Freeman

Triggadale 1, 2 & 3

Tales 4rm Da Dale

FOLLOW ELIJAH R. FREEMAN ON SOCIAL MEDIA

FB:

Elijah R. Freeman

IG:

@the_future_of_urban_fiction

Made in United States
North Haven, CT
20 July 2023

39317543R00124